Lives of the Musicians

David Bowie

Robert Dimery

Laurence King Publishing

LAURENCE KING

Published in 2021 by
Laurence King Publishing Ltd
361–373 City Road
London EC1V 1LR
United Kingdom
T + 44 (0)20 7841 6900
enquiries@laurenceking.com
www.laurenceking.com

A catalogue record for this book is available
from the British Library.

ISBN: 978-1-78627-800-5

Printed in Italy

Laurence King Publishing is committed to ethical
and sustainable production. We are proud participants
in The Book Chain Project®
bookchainproject.com

Cover illustration: Timba Smits

CONTENTS

Do I contradict myself?
Very well then I contradict myself,
(I am large, I contain multitudes.)
Walt Whitman, 'Song of Myself', 1892

Foreword:
Who Can I Be Now?

During the seventies, David Bowie rewrote pop with a bravado and inventiveness that recalled the Beatles at their zenith. With each album he drew a line, moving on to a new sound/voice/look/philosophy for the next release, swerving artistic dead ends. He stayed fresh, changing collaborators as he might change hairstyles and looking to cultural margins and outliers for inspiration. He lived with 'antennae always up', in a phrase coined by Paul McCartney to describe the Beatles. Like them, too, Bowie's work ethic and hit rate were astonishing, especially during the white heat of 1971–7, a period embracing his career highlights *Hunky Dory*, *The Rise and Fall of Ziggy Stardust and the Spiders from Mars*, *Station to Station*, *Low* and *"Heroes"*, as well as the movie *The Man Who Fell to Earth*. He was often accused of being cold and detached, and wrote hardly any love songs, but from 'Five Years' to "Heroes" his catalogue includes a host of anthems born to be sung along to.

For the generations of songwriters who have come after him, Bowie's influence is so ubiquitous as to be practically invisible – 'almost like saying that food is an influence', in St Vincent's words, while Janelle Monaé has spoken of him as 'a part of my musical DNA'. Monaé's 2010 album

The ArchAndroid was part of a conceptual series partly inspired by Fritz Lang's dark cinematic masterpiece *Metropolis*, its protagonist a cosmic messianic figure in a sci-fi dystopia. The parallels with Bowie's imperial seventies phase are plentiful there, and he would have empathized with Monaé's sexual non-conformism, too. Lady Gaga has readily embraced alter egos, and admits to asking herself, 'What would David Bowie do?' when facing an artistic crossroads. In the seventies the British kids who'd seen Bowie performing as Ziggy, a glam-rock peacock, on TV, carried his torch on into punk (Siouxsie Sioux and her Banshees), post-punk (Joy Division), electronica (Gary Numan, the Human League, ABC) and the new romantics (Culture Club, Japan, Spandau Ballet). And how Bowie-esque of Radiohead to follow the all-conquering *OK Computer* (1997) with the fractured electronica of *Kid A* (2000), or make 2007's *In Rainbows* a pay-what-you-want release, experimenting with market practices as others might tamper with a sample.

At the end of an interview with Bowie in 1997, music paper *NME* ran down a list of criticisms levelled at him over the years ('He's piggy-backing on the credibility of more cutting-edge artists; for all his arty rhetoric, he's a hammy Broadway trouper of the Judy Garland school'). Then it revealed that they'd all been taken from its own pages between 1972 and 1980 – Bowie's *anni mirabiles*. In his prime, he never had a fixed identity, as the rock 'n' roll stars before him, such as Elvis Presley or the Rolling Stones, did. They became archetypes, but Bowie was something altogether more elusive and mercurial. 'You never know who you're getting when you photograph an actor,' mused

David Bailey, who shot Bowie in his Ziggy pomp for *Vogue* in 1972. 'And he was always an actor.' Bowie explored different identities, characters that suggested different ways of being and of interpreting the world. Under the guise of an assumed persona, he could experiment, then move on, skirting repetition and staleness. He might wrong-foot his audience, but he'd never bore them. 'One of the principles in rock is that it's the person himself expressing what he really and truly feels,' he observed in 1987. 'And that applies to a lot of artists. But to me it doesn't. It never did.'

Bowie embodied, and relished, contradiction. The alienation and ambiguous sexuality of his most famous creations made him a magnet for those unsure of themselves and their place in the world: outsiders; mavericks. And, naturally, teenagers: the anxiety and isolation that pepper his work endeared him to unsettled adolescents. To a twenty-first century in which the sexual spectrum is considered broader and more nuanced, that seems prescient indeed: the Merriam-Webster Dictionary's word of the year for 2019 was 'they', as a singular personal pronoun used to denote someone of non-binary orientation. And while some dismissed him as a dilettante for cherry-picking from pop and wider pop culture, his magpie tendencies, restlessness and low boredom threshold seem strikingly familiar to us today, increasingly reliant as we are on social media and the internet to satisfy our hunger for stimulation and novelty.

In 2019 London's Design Museum staged a retrospective on the revered filmmaker Stanley Kubrick that featured a tribute to the auteur from another singular director, Mike Leigh. 'In a dozen or so films,' Leigh noted, '[Kubrick] demonstrates his remarkably adventurous versatility, endlessly inspiring us to realize that you can be widely varied in form and content, without ever losing your vision and style, or descending into mere eclecticism.' During Bowie's golden years, that was his everyday working practice. He remained a pop fan all his life, and was sometimes pilloried for his cavalier filching of ideas from other, often younger artists. (*Sounds* magazine sniffily compared much of *Ziggy Stardust* to the work of a 'competent plagiarist'.) But more often than not, he transmuted whatever he pick-pocketed into something that eclipsed the original.

Quite deliberately, Bowie set about collapsing the boundaries between 'high' and 'low' art – 'A cross between Nijinsky and Woolworths,' in his own pithy summation. His interests were broad and catholic. He once said that he was at his happiest reading, and often took a stock of some 1,500 books on tour, redeploying what he'd learned into his songs, spreading the word to his listeners. And if that sometimes led to pidgin philosophy stitched together from eclectic sources, not all of them reliable and some of which he later refuted, that comes with the territory when you're an autodidact. In 2013 he posted a list of 100 life-changing books he'd read, which became part of the touring exhibition *David Bowie Is*. It has been seized on by book clubs, including a Twitter edition overseen by his son. In this, as in his multifaceted music, Bowie's influence lives on.

All that said, for a rock 'n' roll alien who morphed into Halloween Jack of Hunger City, a cold-eyed Aryan aristocrat and the blind prophet Button Eyes, Bowie's beginning was decidedly down to earth …

1

Becoming Bowie

David Robert Jones was born on 8 January 1947 at 40 Stansfield Road in Brixton, south London, his home for the first six years of his life. His father, Haywood Stenton 'John' Jones, worked as general superintendent for the children's charity Barnardo's, and had met David's mother, Peggy (née Margaret Mary Burns), when she was working as a waitress at the Ritz Cinema in Tunbridge, Kent. Both came from previous relationships: John had a daughter, Annette, following an extramarital dalliance; Peggy too strayed from the marital bed, giving birth to a son, Terry, in 1937 and a daughter, Myra Ann, four years later. The atmosphere at home could be strained; Terry often argued with his mother, who had a reputation for being distant and cold, but the young David adored him. The two began sharing a bedroom, although Terry was a teenager by the time his young half-brother started at Stockwell Junior School.

The Joneses moved house several times, eventually winding up in the leafier suburbs of Bromley, in a two-up two-down Edwardian terraced house at 4 Plaistow Grove that backed on to a pub, by which time John had been promoted to Barnardo's PR officer. Terry remained behind in Brixton, then briefly stayed in a box room at the family's new home before beginning his RAF National Service in 1956. David enrolled at Burnt Ash School, where his inherent charisma and vim swiftly won over everyone from his schoolmates to the headmaster, George Lloyd. He also joined a local church choir and the 18th Bromley Cub Pack, where he met George Underwood and Geoff MacCormack, both of whom would become lifelong friends.

To outsiders, the Jones household could come across as strait-laced and chilly. Dana Gillespie, one of David's earliest girlfriends, remembered visiting and being surprised by the lack of conversation and his parents' absolute focus on their blaring TV set. 'I want to get out of here,' he confessed to her afterwards. 'I have to get out of here.' Years later, he'd muse, 'In suburbia you are given the impression that nothing culturally belongs to you. That you are in this sort of wasteland.' Its limbo status, neither the metropolis nor the countryside, bored him, fostered his dreams and gave him something to kick against. It was a restlessness shared by a host of future British pop stars, including Paul Weller, Siouxsie Sioux, Tracey Thorn and Suede's Brett Anderson, all of whom grew up on the fringes of London.

In 1953 John Jones bought a television set so that the family could watch the coronation of Queen Elizabeth II. Scant weeks later, David was glued to the landmark British sci-fi series *The Quatermass Experiment*. The adult Bowie admitted that it scared him stiff but engendered in him an enduring love of science fiction. And its theme tune – 'Mars, the Bringer of War', the opening movement of Gustav Holst's orchestral suite *The Planets* – stuck with him. Some three years later his father brought home an armful of US 45s, still a relatively recent format then (RCA Records had issued the first ones in 1949). Original Stateside releases were a rarity in the UK. The clutch ranged from Fats Domino's easy-rolling R&B and Chuck Berry's teenage rock 'n' roll vignettes to the joyous doo-wop of Frankie Lymon and the Teenagers and the Moonglows. Then David played Little Richard's 'Tutti Frutti'. And that was it: 'I had heard God,' he recalled. 'My heart nearly burst with excitement. I'd never heard anything even resembling this. It filled the room with energy and colour and outrageous defiance.' He said later that at the time his goal was to become one of the four saxophonists he'd seen backing Richard in the 1956 rock 'n' roll flick *The Girl Can't Help It*. For Christmas 1961, his father would buy him a white acrylic Grafton alto sax.

But Richard's explosive music was only half the story; he was also a living, squealing object lesson in grade-A showmanship. George Underwood recalled going to a Little Richard gig at the Woolwich Granada in 1962 with David. At one point, standing on his white grand piano, the rocker began clutching his heart and croaking. Underwood and Jones swapped glances. Richard collapsed and the call went out for a doctor. Then his head rose to the microphone fortuitously positioned near his mouth, and he let rip: 'AWOPBOBALOOBOP ALOPBAMBOOM!' David Jones took note.

Terry Burns provided another vibrant palette of influences. Demobbed from the RAF but not welcome in the Bromley family home, he settled near Beckenham. David's beloved half-brother introduced him to the work of leading Beat writers Allen Ginsberg, Jack Kerouac, Lawrence Ferlinghetti and William Burroughs, along with modern jazz icons such as the bassist Charles Mingus and saxophonists John Coltrane and Eric Dolphy. He uncorked stories about the gigs he'd seen in London's jazz clubs, while his interest in Buddhism also lodged with David, who later claimed that 'Terry probably gave me the greatest education that I could ever have had … He just introduced me to the *outside* things.'[1]

But by now, Terry was also exhibiting troubling symptoms of the mental trauma that was to dog him for the rest of his life. David's mother's side of the family was said to be stricken with the 'Burns curse'; three of her sisters were thought to be mentally troubled, and Bowie himself later noted, with darkly dry wit: 'Everyone says, "Oh yes, my family is quite mad." Mine really is.' It's worth noting, though, that in 2017 his cousin Kristina Amadeus robustly dismissed the idea of genetic schizophrenia in the family. Speaking to Bowie's biographer Dylan Jones, she offered credible alternative explanations for the women's troubled mental states. Her mother, Bowie's aunt Una, suffered a traumatic brain injury at the age of nine and later a nervous breakdown after her husband deserted her; a hospital, unaware of her childhood accident, classified her as schizophrenic. Problems at birth had left David's aunt Nora with learning difficulties, while his aunt Vivienne had been born prematurely, developed tuberculosis and later suffered from clinical depression. Kristina also reported that on leaving the RAF in 1958, Terry said he'd been given mind-altering drugs while serving in Malta and Tripoli, and had entered boxing contests; both may have affected his mental stability.

[1] Italics mine.

In Francis Whately's 2019 documentary *David Bowie: Finding Fame*, she reaffirmed, 'One of the porkies that David perpetuated for a very long time was that he came from a family where insanity seemed to be the norm. And it just wasn't true.'

David's friendship with Underwood continued at Bromley Technical High School. By the early sixties his burgeoning interest in girls was well established and warmly reciprocated, thanks to his charm, waif-like aura and angelic good looks – and despite his wonky teeth, a trademark feature until he had them fixed in the nineties. In 1962 Underwood set up a date with a local schoolgirl named Carol Goldsmith. But David told Underwood that she'd pulled out – so he could move in on her, of course. When Underwood discovered the ruse, he confronted David and punched him; his fist scratched David's left eyeball. He was rushed to Moorfields Eye Hospital, but although he didn't lose his eyesight, the sphincter muscles in that eye were paralysed, leaving the pupil permanently dilated and giving the impression that his left eye was now darker, and green, while his right remained blue. Later, he'd thank Underwood for giving him such an otherworldly feature.

On 16 June 1962 the 15-year-old David debuted with his first band, the Kon-Rads (George Underwood had been their original lead vocalist), at a Tech fete. He played saxophone and contributed occasional vocals, his blond hair sculpted into a luxuriant quiff. The period marks his first experiments with stage pseudonyms, including 'David Jay', 'Luther Jay' and 'Alexis Jay': not as immediately expressive as those dreamed up by manager Larry Parnes for his stable of Brit rock 'n' rollers (Billy Fury, Marty Wilde, Duffy Power et al.), but an early sign that he was trying on the accoutrements of a star. With future Rolling Stones manager Eric Easton as their agent, the group played local low-key socials, and the following year even recorded a demo tape at R.G. Jones in Morden for Easton to tout to Decca Records. 'I Never Dreamed' had a generic Beat group sound; it was rejected by the label and forgotten by the band. But, rediscovered in an old breadbasket in 2018 by Kon-Rad drummer/manager David Hadfield, it fetched nearly £40,000 at auction as the first recording with the then 16-year-old David Jones as a vocalist.

David left Bromley Tech and formal schooling in the summer of 1963 with one O-level, in art. Fortunately, his inspirational teacher Owen Frampton, father of seventies rock pin-up Peter, stepped in. 'He was completely misunderstood by most of my teaching colleagues,' Frampton recalled. 'But in those days cults were unfashionable and David, by the age of 14, was already a cult figure.' Frampton Sr put him in touch with Nevin D. Hirst, a Bond Street advertising agency. In July David joined the company as a 'junior visualizer' – in other words, a cut-and-paste trainee and tea boy.

Although less than committed to his new day job, he picked up key lessons on how to promote and present product. Reportedly, he devoted much of his working day to dreaming up ways to maximize the Kon-Rads' impact – a different image (maybe the Wild West?), perhaps a name change (the Ghost Riders? And he could rename himself Jim Bowie, after the iconic gunfighter played by Richard Widmark in the Western *The Alamo*). He was inventive and prolific, but his schemes never amounted to much, not least because he never settled long enough on one idea. And anyway, the Kon-Rads' shelf life was very nearly up. In October 1963 David had another musical eureka moment when he saw the Rolling Stones at Lewisham Odeon alongside Bo Diddley, the Everly Brothers and his original rock 'n' roll hero, Little Richard. In a move that was to become an enduring trait, he fell heavily for a new sound: R&B and the blues. Unexpectedly, his musical passions were encouraged by his boss at Hirst, a hipster who sent him on regular jaunts to buy LPs from Dobell's Records on Charing Cross Road, a haven for rare imports, which also counted the teenage Eric Clapton as a customer. Further inspired by the pared-down folk songs on Bob Dylan's debut LP, released the previous year, he and Underwood also began performing as the Hooker Brothers.

'All he wanted to do was practise, and listen to tapes or records that he'd got hold of,' remembered Dorothy Bass, a schoolfriend of David's and sometime roadie for another of the scene's young acts, the Pretty Things. 'He would pass a party, or anything up if there was something he needed to do for his music.' In early 1964 he answered an advert in the music paper *Melody Maker* from a trio in Fulham in search of a vocalist and, along with Underwood, wound up joining the King Bees. With admirable chutzpah – and his father's help – he wrote to a successful businessman, John Bloom, advising him: 'If you can sell my group the way you sell washing machines, you'll be on to a winner.' Amused, though not convinced, Bloom passed the letter on to Leslie Conn, a showbiz manager. It worked: Conn got the King Bees signed up to make their debut disc – albeit on Vocalion, a lowly subsidiary of Decca Records. Despite respectable radio and TV promotion (including *Juke Box Jury* and *The Beat Room*), the single 'Liza Jane', credited to 'Davie Jones with the King Bees', sank without trace, but David did get to make his TV debut with the band in June 1964 on TV's must-see music show *Ready, Steady Go!* He sported a leather waistcoat and suede Robin Hood-style boots.

Now he and Conn devised an audacious new publicity stunt. Tapping into contemporary hissing about long-haired men – David's carefully combed locks now overran his collar, Stones-style – on 2 November he appeared in a *London Evening News & Star* article. Written by future *Virgin Soldiers* author Leslie Thomas (a former Barnardo's boy who'd been brought on board by John Jones), it presented the teenager as founder of the non-existent International League for the Preservation of Animal Filament. It garnered him an appearance on the BBC's *Tonight* show later that month, flanked by seven similarly hirsute youths, now redubbed the Society for the Prevention of Cruelty to Long-Haired Men. 'I think we're all fairly tolerant,' he tells the balding Cliff Michelmore, who plays along amiably, 'but for the last two years we've had comments like "Darling" and "Can I carry your handbag?" … I think it's just had to stop." Harmless TV fluff, but it kept David Jones's profile, such as it was, simmering.

By 1964 he was spending more and more time at La Gioconda, a wood-panelled coffee bar at 9 Denmark Street. Musicians gravitated there to swap stories over a brew and a cigarette while scouring the music papers for auditions or gigs. Denmark Street itself was London's Tin Pan Alley, born at the turn of the century, when its affordable rents and proximity to the West End theatres made it a haven for sheet-music publishers and industry professionals, such as arrangers. At barely 100 metres long, you could walk it in half a minute, but Denmark Street accommodated instrument shops, managers, agents and music publishers, whose offices spilled around the corner on to Charing Cross Road (where the Beatles' publisher Dick James held court), with booking agents nearby too. Both *NME* and *Melody Maker* were based there. If you wanted to make a demo record or single, at no. 4 was the tiny recording studio Regent Sound, its walls lined with eggbox cartons for soundproofing. But that unpromising space counted the Rolling Stones (who recorded their first LP there in 1964), the Kinks and the Yardbirds among its clients, and later the likes of Jimi Hendrix, Elton John and Black Sabbath. Central Sound Studio, another small set-up, was on the first floor next door to La Gioconda, and Tin Pan Alley Studios was in a basement at no. 22.

Back then, Soho was heaven for mods, young sharp dressers who adored R&B, soul and ska (although the name was short for 'modernists', derived from the modern jazz that the original mods of the late fifties had favoured). Within easy walking distance were venues such as the Marquee, the Flamingo Club and La Discotheque – all on Wardour Street. Best of all was the Scene, in Ham Yard, where David would play with his next band. To sustain themselves on marathon clubbing benders, mods popped amphetamine ('speed') pills. In his 2002 memoir *Black Vinyl White Powder*, manager Simon Napier-Bell remembered the Flamingo as a good place to score Benzedrine, sold by American servicemen for around sixpence a tablet, while Drinamyl (an amphetamine-and-barbiturate mix, also known as Blues) was the drug of choice at the Scene. 'I used to go to an all-night café in Soho,' recalled Napier-Bell, 'that served pick-me-up sandwiches sprinkled with pills like salt and pepper.'

It was at La Gioconda in 1964 that David Jones became acquainted with another young singer under Conn's care: Mark Feld, whom Conn had also come across there. Feld was already a known mod about town: aged just 15, he'd been profiled in *Town* magazine in September 1962, photographed by the great Don McCullin; he boasted elfin good looks and popped with ambition. Feld and Jones once spent a morning repainting Conn's office, in part-compensation for their not making him any money, egging each other on with how spectacularly successful they were going to become, a conversation they'd repeat in Soho's cafes, nursing a cup of coffee for hours. In time, they'd raid the bins of Carnaby Street menswear shops together, filtering out promising gear. Their paths were to criss-cross intermittently during the decade, and a (mostly) friendly rivalry developed between them.

Ambitious, unsentimental and pragmatic, the two regularly reappraised their musical identities during the sixties as they sought to engineer their lucky break. Feld started out in the vein of Cliff Richard, then switched to folk music as peak-capped Toby Tyler before renaming himself Marc Bolan, openly aping Bob Dylan on the breezy flop 'The Wizard' in 1966, featuring Jimmy Page on guitar. Eventually, his songwriting talent did attract a sympathetic manager in Napier-Bell. He placed the elfin guitarist with pop-art proto-punks John's Children, whose anarchic stage show saw them thrown off a tour with the Who, and for whom he wrote the controversial 'Desdemona', which the BBC banned. He went on to form his own rock band, Tyrannosaurus Rex, who bombed on their live debut as an electric four-piece. But, slimmed down to an acoustic duo of just Bolan and the percussionist Steve Peregrin Took, they began to gain traction, their folky Tolkeinesque tales winning them a fanbase among students and the counterculture, and attracting invaluable support from the DJ John Peel.

In 1964, however, both Feld and Jones were still directionless. The King Bees swiftly went the same way as the Kon-Rads. In July, David abruptly told a stunned Underwood, 'I've decided to break the band up – and I've found another band.' Conn had introduced him to the Manish Boys, a brass-heavy R&B outfit who briefly joined a package tour alongside the Kinks in December 1964. The Kinks' breakthrough singles – 'You Really Got Me' and 'All Day and All of the Night' – were powerhouse pop, and Dave Davies's exhilarating, distorted lead guitar breaks a harbinger of heavy rock. But his brother Ray would prove to be a subtler and more intriguing influence on David, most obviously in the deft vignettes that he wove into his songs, but perhaps also in his nuanced vocals and the hint of camp in his coy gestures.

The Kinks' producer, Shel Talmy, had made a name for himself with the punchy, highly compressed sound he created for bands in the studio (he also oversaw the Who's crucial early singles and their explosive debut album). Now he was recruited for the Manish Boys' new single, a cover of Bobby 'Blue' Bland's 'I Pity the Fool'. The arrangement married a sleepwalking beat to fulsome brass, with

David already sounding like a promising vocalist. Talmy also gave him studio time to work up demo material. The producer dismissed the results ('It was weird music'), but the Manish Boys' single gave David his first credit as a songwriter, on the B-side 'Take My Tip' – also the first of his songs to be covered, by Kenny Miller. The session guitarist Talmy recruited for the recording was Jimmy Page, who complimented the band on their performance, but assured them that 'I Pity the Fool' wouldn't be a hit. (It stiffed after its release in March 1965.) More generously, Page gave David a riff he'd written, which was stored away for future use.

During the summer of 1965, a chance meeting gave David another experience that he'd draw on later. Rocker Vince Taylor's square-jawed good looks, black pompadour and crazy-man-crazy dancing had set Soho's 2I's coffee bar alight in the late fifties. His wayward vocals guaranteed he'd never make it, but he did pen the raucous 'Brand New Cadillac', later covered by the Clash. Wearing a leather suit à la Gene Vincent, he grew into a cult hero in France in the early sixties, but then developed a taste for LSD that gave him messianic delusions: he became convinced that he was Jesus Christ. When David bumped into Taylor at La Gioconda, the latter was dressed in a long robe and sandals, but the teenager was unfazed and the two struck up a meandering conversation taking in religion, UFOs and the myth of Atlantis. Afterwards they strolled towards Tottenham Court Road Tube station. Taylor laid a map on the ground and began pointing out landing sites for flying saucers and hidden caches of money. The day registered deeply with the young singer: Vince Taylor would slot into the jigsaw puzzle that became his most famous creation.

2

Of Mods and Mime

The hitless Manish Boys split in 1965, but David wasn't unemployed for long. Spotted in La Gioconda by two members of Margate outfit the Lower Third, who mistook him for the Yardbirds singer Keith Relf, he was invited to audition for them at Wardour Street's La Discotheque. David took a new friend for moral support – Steve Marriott, whom he'd met while rehearsing with the Manish Boys. Marriott was clearly the better vocalist, but David's assurance impressed the band more.

The Manish Boys had had the unkempt appearance of Stones wannabes but with the Lower Third, David Jones became a mod. His flowing locks were sculpted at Ivan's of Queensway into a fashionable bouffant crop with side parting on the left. In Jonathon Green's oral history *Days in the Life*, original scenester David May reflected that 'Mods were always intellectual. There was always a large gay element in it. On Saturday afternoon we'd go to get our hair done in the women's hairdressers … But underneath this, one did read Camus. *The Outsider*, there it was, it explained an awful lot.' Much of this would filter into David's future mindset, and an interest in existentialist literature aligned neatly with the Beatnik culture that his half-brother Terry had already introduced him to. Mods were narcissists, obsessing over sartorial details (the length of the vents in one's jacket, its button count) that would be understood and appreciated only by others in the know. They were males attracting a largely male gaze. Many mods wore make-up, too; David later recalled the shock and thrill of seeing just such a well-turned-out young man wearing eyeshadow on the train up to London one day.

With the Lower Third, he pushed his ideas and songs harder than before, and his energy and determination made him the outfit's natural leader. He began encouraging them to toughen up their sound along the lines of the Who, whose intense live set he'd already caught; they also worked up a steaming take on the Yardbirds' 'Wish You Would', on which he deftly mimicked Relf's delivery. With Shel Talmy, they recorded the single 'You've Got a Habit of Leaving' for the EMI subsidiary Parlophone, the Beatles' label. Audibly indebted to the Who and the Kinks, it was another of his self-penned songs – as was the B-side, 'Baby Loves that Way' – and another flop. And imagine how the rest of the Lower Third felt when they saw that the label on the disc credited only 'Davy Jones'. By now, Leslie Conn had lost interest in him, and Mark Feld too, but the enterprising David already had a replacement in mind in the form of Ralph Horton. Another connection from La Gioconda, he worked at the Kings booking agency next door at no. 7, and had been the Moody Blues' road manager.

The quartet gigged regularly during the second half of 1965, playing south-coast seaside resorts as well as key London venues the Marquee and the 100 Club. They even supported the Who, although their unoriginality was painfully apparent. When the Lower Third were sound-checking before their first gig with the Who, at Bournemouth in August 1965, Pete Townshend walked in. Afterwards, he asked whose song they'd just played. 'It's mine,' David told him. 'That's a shame,' Townshend replied. 'Sounds like my stuff.'

Badly in need of funds and an experienced partner for his new venture, Horton sought out Simon Napier-Bell, who recalled: 'He said that if I were to agree to come in on the management, he would allow me to have sex with his young protégé. I had no idea whether the protégé was in on the proposition or not.' Napier-Bell turned Horton down, but the latter also approached Kenneth Pitt, a seasoned industry professional who'd handled PR for Bob Dylan's UK tour in 1965; other clients included Frank Sinatra (to whom he was 'my man in London') and Duke Ellington. Pitt declined too, although he did advise Horton that another Davy Jones, the future Monkee, was already creating a stir on Broadway in Lionel Bart's Dickensian musical *Oliver!* A name change might be in order. A couple of days later Pitt received a gushing letter from Horton, thanking him for his advice and announcing that Davy Jones would henceforth be known as David Bowie, a pseudonym harking back to his Kon-Rad days.

EMI and Talmy dropped the band, but their singer remained robustly upbeat. Flying in the face of pop logic, he introduced revved-up covers of 'Chim Chim Cher-ee' (from Disney's *Mary Poppins*) and Holst's 'Mars, the Bringer of War' into the Lower Third's live sets. Their guitarist Denis Taylor remembered much of Bowie's material as distinctly downbeat, even 'morbid'. 'The London Boys' epitomizes the crossroads his music had come to; set to a sparse arrangement, the lyrics describe an unsettled youth arriving in London and embracing the mod lifestyle of fast living, fashion and pills, only to become lonelier than ever. Such character sketches would typify Bowie's first solo album. 'I think I preferred David as a mod,' Pitt admitted later. 'He summed up mod culture with some of his early songs, because he was so observant. He wanted to sing about the mods he saw hanging around Wardour Street.' But, like Ray Davies, Bowie was writing as an outsider – a suburbanite on the edge of the action, not at its heart.

The band ended 1965 with triumphant gigs at Paris's Club Drouot. But despite his music business connections, Horton was clearly struggling. And in addition to running up debts, he had driven a wedge between Bowie and the rest of the Lower Third, not least by bringing the singer back from gigs in his Jaguar, leaving the rest to take the converted ambulance that served as their van. More positively, he secured them a new record contract, this time with Pye Records and Tony Hatch lined up to produce. Their next single was Bowie's best yet.

Revisiting it with a rattlingly good version for VH1's *Storytellers* in 1999, Bowie played down 'Can't Help Thinking about Me', highlighting 'two of the worst lines I've ever written'. But its ruminative narrative – a kitchen-sink tale of leaving home after an unnamed disgrace – is intriguing, while the title encapsulates mod narcissism and teenage self-obsession and subverts traditional pop sensibilities ('me', rather than 'you'). Credited to 'David Bowie with the Lower Third', the single was released on 14 January 1966, reaching No. 34 on *Melody Maker*'s chart, but missing the important *Record Retailer* Top 40 altogether. By contrast, Bowie's friend Marriott and his band the Small Faces had already scored a UK Top 20 hit with 'Whatcha Gonna Do about It'. In 1966 they'd enjoy four British Top 10 hits. David Bowie was lagging behind.

By now, Horton had begun withholding wages (for 'expenses'), forcing Denis Taylor and bassist Graham Rivens to live in the band van for want of rent money. On 29 January, following a regular Saturday afternoon gig at the Marquee, they were told they wouldn't be paid to play Bromley's Bromel Club that evening. There was a showdown outside the venue. Horton, who drove up with Bowie in his car, refused to compromise. Bowie declined to step in. And that was that.

The single had attracted decent reviews, and on 4 March Bowie performed it on *Ready, Steady, Go!* with a new band, the Buzz. They backed Bowie on his next dud, too, the unremarkable 'Do Anything You Say', although by April they'd secured a residency at the Marquee, where for a couple of months Sunday afternoons were given over to a 'Bowie Showboat', which saw the singer dip into West End shows and cabaret as well as rock 'n' roll. Horton invited Kenneth Pitt down on 17 April, and this time he was convinced, the clincher most probably coming when the room went dark, save for a spotlight on Bowie, who delivered an impassioned reading of the Anthony Newley show-stopper 'What Kind

of Fool Am I?'[1] from the 1961 musical *Stop the World –
I Want to Get Off*. Back at Pitt's Marylebone flat afterwards,
they struck a deal.

Pitt was perhaps most truly at home working in cabaret
and light entertainment, worlds more naturally associated
with the theatre than with rock 'n' roll. Accordingly, his
tenure as Bowie's manager has been seen as attempting
to coerce the singer in that direction. But that's unfair on
Pitt, who had worked on publicity for Jerry Lee Lewis in
the fifties, as well as managing the band Manfred Mann
until 1965. A more charitable interpretation might be that
he saw there was far more to David Bowie than simply
a halfway-decent R&B singer. Bowie himself was clearly
open-minded about his career. In February 1966 he was
telling *Melody Maker*, 'I want to act. I'd like to do character
parts. I think it takes a lot to become somebody else.' Fast-
forward to *NME* of 11 October 1969, and he'd broadened
his canvas: 'I'm determined to be an entertainer … clubs,
cabaret, concerts, the lot.'

Once he'd paid off the considerable debts Horton had
accrued, Pitt set about refocusing Bowie's recording career
as a solo artist. There was no mileage in staying at Pye –
the Tony Hatch-produced 'I Dig Everything' was another
failure. Instead, in October Pitt sent Bowie and the Buzz
into R.G. Jones studios to demo material that heralded an

---

[1] Some sources suggest that the song was 'You'll Never Walk Alone',
from the musical *Carousel* (1945). Either way, Bowie had opted for
heart-on-the-sleeve melodrama, placing him squarely outside the
sixties rock fraternity and far closer to the world of conventional
show business.

altogether different direction: a reworking of 'The London Boys' alongside a couple of odd but distinctive new tracks, 'Please Mr Gravedigger' and 'Rubber Band'. Pitt and Hatch were confident in Bowie's talent, but aware of the esoteric nature of his songs, and they knew he was never going to be an overnight star. Nevertheless, his demos won a contract with Decca's recently formed progressive subsidiary Deram, and in the autumn of 1966, his focus renewed by the new deal and the prospect of his debut LP, he embarked on a hugely productive bout of songwriting. That December he made his debut as a Deram artist with 'Rubber Band'/'The London Boys'.

Bowie's personal charm was an enduring factor in his success, enabling him to talk musicians into trying out his outlandish ideas, or session musicians to play for a reduced fee (or no fee at all). He used it to great effect with journalists – spectacularly so in the seventies, but in the preceding decade, too. *Disc* magazine's Penny Valentine was an early and enthusiastic champion. *Melody Maker*'s Chris Welch recalled that she seemed lovestruck with Bowie – although he added, tellingly, 'She did mention how he wouldn't stop ringing her up.' Ditto Decca's chairman, Hugh Mendl, who confessed to a 'minor obsession' with him. *NME*'s Charles Shaar Murray, who regularly interviewed Bowie in the seventies, spoke of harbouring 'a kind of platonic man-love for him', and of his use of charm as a 'weapon'. Needless to say, Bowie enchanted Horton and Pitt too (the latter became his sole manager in April 1967). Both were of fluid sexuality, and as a young, amenable artist with energy and talent to spare, it's no wonder Bowie impressed them. Despite his many liaisons with girls, his sexual preferences were by no means set, or clear to those around him: 'Nobody at that time knew he was gay except for me and Ralph Horton,' Pitt later stated. 'David would have gone to any extreme at that time to avoid it being known.' One of the Kon-Rads, Alan Dodds, recalled Bowie telling the band he was bisexual in the early sixties, but couldn't recall any evidence to back it up. Bowie evidently didn't come across as wholly heterosexual, anyway: 'We thought Marc Bolan was gay,' Pete Townshend observed. 'We thought David Bowie was gay. We thought all the cool people were gay.'

Townshend himself benefited hugely from a relationship with his own mentor. In the mid-sixties he briefly lived with the band's co-manager, Christopher 'Kit' Lambert, in the spare room of the latter's Belgravia office-cum-apartment. Lambert's father, Constant, was a composer and conductor of some renown, and Kit opened the receptive Townshend's eyes to culture outside rock 'n' roll and jazz, as well as acting as an invaluable sounding board and perceptive critic. Likewise Kenneth Pitt. During the preparation and release of the *David Bowie* LP, the singer was still based at Plaistow Grove, although a combination of his night-time writing routines and the reappearance of Terry Burns in the cramped family home made the situation stressful for everyone. John Jones, who kept in touch with Pitt to monitor the progress of his son's career, would have made that clear. So when Pitt offered to have Bowie live with him in his flat at 39 Manchester Street, it provided welcome relief all round. Bowie moved in June 1967, and his new home gave him access to Pitt's library, which opened his eyes to the oeuvre of Expressionist painter Egon Schiele, Christopher Isherwood's novels set in Weimar-era Berlin, and works by Oscar Wilde and Aubrey Beardsley. As a mentor-manager, Pitt had something of the conscientiousness and personal affection for Bowie that Brian Epstein had for the Beatles, and Kit Lambert for Pete Townshend. All three managers were of a different generation from their charges, though, and didn't fully embrace the emerging youth culture of which their charges were leading lights.

'At a time when being gay was illegal,' Simon Napier-Bell told the *Guardian*'s Alexis Petridis in 2012, 'and the only way to live as an out gay man was to work in the theatre or as a hairdresser, pop management offered a new opportunity.' In the late fifties the gay Svengali Larry Parnes had groomed a succession of handsome young male singers for success, realigning their appeal from older homosexual men such as himself to young teenage girls and setting a precedent for the following decade. For Napier-Bell, the very fact that so many pop managers of the time were gay had other major advantages: 'It was gay managers, and their friends in fashion and media, who were chiefly responsible for creating the image of British youth culture that was being sold around the world,' he observed in *Black Vinyl White Powder*. Several notable managers of the sixties, including Epstein, Robert Stigwood (who managed the Bee Gees and Cream), Napier-Bell (the Yardbirds, John's Children, Marc Bolan) and Lambert, were gay or bisexual. So was Bowie's previous mentor Ralph Horton. With homosexual acts a crime in the UK until the Sexual Offences Act of 1967, and homosexuality perceived by many for years to come as a social stigma, they kept their personal lives as private as possible – although that didn't stop the sometimes incautious Epstein from being blackmailed.

Bowie's own sexual experimentation was hardly novel for the times. 'I just thought that if people wanted to sleep together they should just be able to, and they shouldn't be prevented by Catholic morality,' observed Richard Neville, of counterculture magazine *Oz*, to Jonathon Green in the late eighties. It's useful to set against that the artist Nicola Lane's comment, again to Green, that 'There was a lot of misery. Relationship miseries: ghastly, ghastly jealousy, although there was supposed to be no jealousy, no possessiveness. What it meant was that men fucked around.' To what extent Bowie considered himself genuinely gay is a moot point. As the sixties wore on – or at least the sixties as experienced by a select few – sexuality became less defined, and several leading pop stars flirted with the boundaries. Like Bowie, the Kinks' Dave Davies enjoyed selected gay flings (with *Ready Steady Go!* presenter Michael Aldred, among others), although for the most part both were voraciously heterosexual. Inspired by his manager Andrew Loog Oldham, a straight man who delighted in camp mannerisms, Mick Jagger became an increasingly flamboyant and effeminate figure as the decade wore on. And he wasn't alone: witness Davies in braided Charles II-style coat and frills, his voluptuous hair parted at the centre, performing 'Death of a Clown' on BBC's *Top of the Pops* in 1967. Or the Small Faces' transformation from mods in sharp suits and buttoned-up shirts in 1965 to paisley-wearing dandies within a couple of years.

David Bowie, the album, had the misfortune to be released in the UK just days after the Beatles' *Sgt Pepper's Lonely Hearts Club Band*, but its chances of chart success were always slim. Overall, the subject matter and arrangements are too sentimental to convince. Music hall and vaudeville are audible touchstones, although other contemporary writers (Lennon/McCartney, Ray Davies) handled the same sources with more elan. There are downbeat vignettes, usually set in the past, in the shape of the 'Little Bombardier' (an ex-soldier whose kindness towards children is misinterpreted) and the cross-dressing female combatant in the comic 'She's Got Medals'. 'Uncle Arthur' remains tied to the maternal apron strings even after marriage. The chirpy 'Love You Till Tuesday' is offset by 'Please Mr Gravedigger', featuring only a vocal and sound effects, in which a child-murderer watches the titular figure at work and plans to kill him. In 'Join the Gang', as with 'The London Boys', the counterculture is parodied for its perceived shallowness – classic sixties Bowie, wanting to be accepted but too individualistic to give himself to any one movement. At the dawn of the rock era, the album contrarily eschews guitars in favour of woodwind and brass (the tuba is the lead instrument on 'Rubber Band', a marching tune). Still, there are hints of the Bowie to come in the messiahs and fascists of 'We Are Hungry Men', while his fledgling interest in Buddhism emerges in 'Silly Boy Blue'.

Then there's 'The Laughing Gnome'. Probably influenced (as was 'Little Bombardier') by Syd Barrett, who wrote 'The Gnome' for the first Pink Floyd LP, it preceded *David Bowie* in April 1967 as a non-album single, and became one of his *bêtes noires*. Its speeded-up comedy vocal interjections and grimace-worthy puns won few fans, although there's much to admire in the neat arrangement. A re-release in 1973, when Bowie's star was triumphantly in the ascendant, would reach No. 6 in the UK. In 1967, though, it stiffed, as did the LP.

Speaking in 1993, Kenneth Pitt recalled that when Bowie arrived at Deram, 'The man who was in charge of the album department said to me, "This is the greatest thing that's come here since Tony Newley."' The epitome of the all-round entertainer that Pitt thought Bowie might become, Anthony Newley was a composer, singer, and stage and screen actor. He notched up two UK No. 1s among 12 UK Top 40 hits from 1959 to 1962, while his credits with his regular writing partner Leslie Bricusse included the lyrics for the Bond theme 'Goldfinger' and 'Feeling Good', immortalized by Nina Simone; the two also wrote the musical *Stop the World – I Want to Get Off*, starring Newley. In 1960 he devised the surreal TV series *The Strange World of Gurney Slade*, in which he played a character in a TV show, and which broke the 'fourth wall' to address the viewer directly. Too odd for prime-time audiences, it lasted only six episodes. Bowie loved it, though, and in his later sixties recordings consciously affected Newley's delivery, its cockney twang and emotive vibrato.

In late 1966 Pitt returned from a business trip to New York, where he'd visited Andy Warhol's studio, the Factory. There he met Lou Reed, the singer in a band Warhol was promoting, and was given a white-label acetate of their debut album: *The Velvet Underground and Nico*. Bowie adored it. During one of the Buzz's shows at the Marquee, the singer had met Bob Flag, a saxophonist in the Riot Squad. They met again at La Gioconda, and when Flag revealed that his outfit was looking for a new vocalist, Bowie jumped at the chance and ensured that the Velvets' 'Waiting for the Man', Reed's ode to scoring heroin, joined the set. 'Not only was I to cover [a] Velvets' song before anyone else in the world,' he later declared gleefully, 'I actually did it before the album came out. Now that's the essence of mod.'

Another key element in the Bowie arsenal came in the form of the fledgling producer Tony Visconti, an American musician who'd arrived in London in April 1967 and within months had worked with Procol Harum and the Move (the string arrangement on the latter's UK No. 2 'Flowers in the Rain' is his). Visconti had introduced Marc Bolan's folk-rock duo Tyrannosaurus Rex to the music publisher Essex Music, and one day its owner, David Platz, invited him to the office to hear the work of another of their writers: David Bowie. Visconti admired the eclecticism of Bowie's debut LP; tellingly, he thought of it in terms of an aural CV, which had been precisely Pitt's intention. Platz had Bowie waiting in an adjoining room, and he and the producer quickly bonded over a shared interest in music, Tibetan Buddhism, books (particularly sci-fi) and film, especially of the art-house variety. They spent the afternoon together, even popping into a King's Road cinema to watch Roman Polanski's *Knife in the Water*.

Bowie's debut LP drew another formative influence into his life. The dancer and mime artist Lindsay Kemp had been playing its track 'When I Live My Dream' at the start of his latest production, *Clowns Hour*, in the Little Theatre

Club off St Martin's Lane. Kemp had been introduced to the record by a secretary at his agency ('She was a mutual friend but I think [Bowie] was probably going out with her. He went out with most people'). He was struck by Bowie's voice, which reminded him not only of Newley but also of the Belgian artist Jacques Brel. Bowie already knew of Brel: one of his on-off paramours, the singer Lesley Duncan, had dated Scott Walker and often played Walker's versions of Brel songs when Bowie was around.

Bowie had soon enrolled at the dancer's studio, where – in Kemp's words – 'I taught him to dance and I taught him how to communicate, how to express himself through his body.' In Kemp, Bowie found a key to a new world of art and allure, and became captivated by the older man's enthusiasm for Japanese kabuki performance, which was to have an impact on his own future stagecraft. An ancient Japanese form of dance/drama, kabuki blends ritual with erotica, incorporating rapid costume changes and symbolic make-up that switches with one's character. It also involves androgyny: its original all-female casts (*onna kabuki*) provoked such sexual frisson among audiences that they were replaced by teenage males (*wakashu*), who elicited an even wilder response. Kemp also shared with Bowie his love of silent movies, the Theatre of the Absurd and the works of Jean Genet. And Kemp himself was an object lesson in living as though one's existence were itself a performance: 'His day-to-day life was the most theatrical thing I'd ever seen,' Bowie reflected in 1997. 'Everything I thought Bohemia probably was, he was living.' The two became lovers, although Kemp swiftly learned that Bowie was no monogamist; when the two toured with Kemp's show *Pierrot in Turquoise*, Bowie bed-hopped with the costume designer Natasha Korniloff.

In January 1968 Kemp and Bowie were filming *The Pistol Shot*, based on an Anton Chekhov play, for the BBC. Kemp choreographed the show and had recruited Hermione Farthingale, a striking classically trained dancer with strawberry-blonde hair. Before the month was out, she and Bowie were in love ('It took maybe five minutes, maximum,' she recalled in 2019), and by August, he'd moved into her South Kensington house-share at 22 Clareville Grove. His next musical excursion gave him the chance to spend even more time with his new soulmate.

Along with the guitarist John 'Hutch' Hutchinson (whom he knew from the Buzz), Bowie and Farthingale formed Feathers, a 'multimedia' trio embracing music, poetry and dance. Their sets included covers of Brel's 'Amsterdam' and 'My Death', both of which Bowie would revisit as a solo artist. Although he didn't release an album in 1968, he put the time to good use. 'He was learning how to put a song together,' Underwood remembers. 'He was putting in so much practice, his learning process suddenly took a big curve upwards.' But in early 1969 Bowie's relationship with Farthingale ended abruptly. The catalyst came when she was offered the part of a dancer in the movie musical *Song of Norway*. 'He was clearly going somewhere,' she reflected some 50 years later, 'and I didn't think I was going to tread that path with him.' Bowie had always made it a policy to seize the next career opportunity when it arose, and Farthingale had ambitions of her own, although their split left both of them heartbroken. But before they parted, the two collaborated with Hutch on a new project that Pitt had dreamed up, one that would finally give David Bowie a hit single.

3
Lift-off

L ove You Till Tuesday (1969) was a half-hour promotional film featuring David Bowie's songs, another
of Kenneth Pitt's attempts to demonstrate the
breadth of his client's talent. Bowie revisited a handful
of tracks from his debut album of 1967 and devised
'The Mask' – a morbid mime piece about the price of
fame – along with several new compositions, including
the children's ditty 'When I'm Five'.[1] And a curious song
about an astronaut.

This new composition had considerable musical input
from Hutch (who briefly formed a duo with Bowie after
Feathers dissolved), introducing abstract, 'floating' chords
that Bowie himself might not have thought of. Marc Bolan
claimed to have told Bowie to sing it in the style of the Bee
Gees, whose first UK hits were melancholy anthems. But
Bowie gave the singular contribution on a Stylophone,
a pocket-sized electronic instrument with a distinctive
buzzing timbre, probably given to him by Bolan (or possibly
Pitt; accounts vary). The lyrics, too, were more completely

---

[1] Bowie's empathy for children, and the way they warmed to him, was
apparent to those around him. Mike Vernon, who produced his debut
LP, characterized Bowie as 'singing songs that ... appeared to be written
by children'.

his, as was the song's title, a twist on that of Stanley Kubrick's classic film *2001: A Space Odyssey* of the year before.

Hutch had a wife, Denise, and young son to support, and eventually headed back home to Scarborough, so it was as a solo artist that Bowie took 'Space Oddity' to the Mercury Philips label. He'd met Mercury's Assistant European Director of Artists and Repertoire, a charismatic and flamboyant Chinese-American from San Francisco named Calvin Lee, at a party a couple of years before. Tony Visconti felt that Bowie's friendship with Lee encouraged the singer to become more extravagant; certainly, among his idiosyncratic features, Lee wore a shimmery silvery-red 'love jewel' disc on his forehead that Bowie would adapt for his most famous alter ego a few years later. Unbeknown to Pitt, in early 1969 Lee was pushing Bowie hard to his boss, Lou Reizner. Indeed, in almost a parody of sixties sexual free-for-alls, Bowie and Lee were having an affair, while Lee was simultaneously in a relationship with Mary Angela Barnett, a young American born in Cyprus – and herself Reizner's love interest. She and Bowie finally met via Lee when the trio went out for a Chinese meal, followed by a trip to the Speakeasy club. Bowie returned with Barnett to her Paddington flat, marking the start of four years in which her can-do attitude, humour and chutzpah drove him on. 'She was outspoken, had courage like you wouldn't believe,' Visconti affirmed in the documentary *David Bowie: Finding Fame* in 2019. 'Angie was the one who made things happen.' The producer Ken Scott, although adamant that her musical influence on Bowie was negligible, also believed that her natural flamboyance rubbed off on Bowie. Smart, cultured and ambitious, she had hopes of finding stardom herself as a film actress; the dashing of those hopes doubtless played its part in the ultimate disintegration of their relationship.

Nevertheless, a few weeks earlier Bowie had met another new partner, Mary Finnigan, while visiting a friend who lived in the top flat of her block in Beckenham. (Ironically, she'd been to the same Swiss finishing school as Angie Barnett.) Sunbathing in her garden, Finnigan had become captivated by the sound of a 12-string guitar playing from above, and called out to the musician ('a pale, thin face framed by a halo of blond hair'). By April 1969 he had moved in with her and her two young children – while continuing to see Barnett – and would remain with her for six months. Before long they'd set up a folk club in the back room of a local pub, the Three Tuns, where he could perform; by the end of May it had been renamed the Beckenham Arts Lab. It gave him a regular platform for his songs, but also offered the opportunity to share his enthusiasm for mime and visual arts in what he hoped would create a fertile creative environment. The climax of his sets was now 'Space Oddity', and he recorded the definitive version on 20 June 1969 at Trident Studios in Soho, with Rick Wakeman – then a session musician and two years away from joining prog-rockers Yes – on Mellotron. Visconti turned down the chance to produce the track, feeling that it was a gimmicky cash-in on the NASA *Apollo 11* launch scheduled for July. He passed it on to a delighted colleague, Gus Dudgeon, who'd engineered *David Bowie*.

First heard over the PA at the Rolling Stones' free gig at Hyde Park on 5 July, 'Space Oddity' had a trajectory that was far from smooth. Despite an enthusiastic response from critics, sales slowed depressingly quickly after it reached No. 48 in the UK. Doubtless, sensitivity about a song involving an astronaut drifting off into space discouraged radio play in the month of NASA's launch. After the astronauts had landed safely, however, things improved, partly because of strident efforts by Lee. ('He promoted the fuck out of it,' according to Visconti. 'He was all over the place, pushing like crazy. He was unpaid as well, as far as I know'.) Philips' dynamic new marketing director, Olav Wyper, also worked the single hard, taking advantage of a three-week lack of new releases to focus his combined promotions, marketing and sales teams on 'Space Oddity'. Gratifyingly, the single rose again, to peak at No. 5.

Visconti had returned to the fold on 16 July to oversee the accompanying album, confusingly also titled *David Bowie*, like his debut (but later reissued in the UK as *Space Oddity*). Alongside him was Ken Scott, at the time an engineer, who'd already served on the Beatles' *Magical Mystery Tour* EP and 'White Album', and Jeff Beck's *Truth*. 'Cygnet Committee' lays into the counterculture and was partly a kiss-off to the apathy Bowie had sensed among the crowd at Beckenham Arts Lab; there was too much spectating and not enough artistic involvement, he felt, and within a month he was toning down his involvement in it. 'Unwashed and Slightly Dazed' offers the first evidence of Bowie the rocker and an acknowledgement of the fact that others might see him as a freak, while in 'Janine' he explores the idea of multiple selves. 'Letter to Hermione' is his first straightforward love song, a real rarity in his work, and reveals his vulnerable side;

the departed Farthingale is also the subject of the poignant 'An Occasional Dream'. By contrast, the anxiety that haunts much of Bowie's work emerges in 'Wild Eyed Boy from Freecloud', the tale of an innocent soul condemned to hang.

In late July, aware of other industry figures now competing for his client's attention, Pitt flew with Bowie to a couple of music festivals in Malta and Italy. Bowie performed 'When I Live My Dream', won a statuette at the Festival Internazionale del Disco, and returned happy and tanned. Unbeknown to him, however, his father had become gravely ill. On hearing the news, Bowie rushed to Plaistow Grove to be with him, but on 5 August John Jones died of pneumonia. His son was devastated. Although Bowie never felt truly loved by his mother, his father was a warmer presence. Jones Sr had supported his son financially and, although apprehensive about his son's career choice, liaised closely with Pitt over his progress. (Like his father, Bowie was a lifelong chain-smoker, initially opting for John's choice of filterless Player's Weights before progressing to Gitanes, Gauloise Disque Bleu and Marlboro Reds.) The loss of his father would inform the bleakness and uncertainty of Bowie's third album.

A scant five days after his father's funeral, Bowie played the biggest gig of his life yet, the Beckenham Free Festival, held at the Croydon Road Recreation Ground. He was initially upbeat, but recent events understandably soured his mood as the day progressed, and he reportedly snapped at the organizers (including Finnigan), calling them 'materialistic assholes' as they counted up the takings. But his song 'Memory of a Free Festival' provided a touching memento of the day, celebrating the communal oneness of the times (the original Woodstock Festival was taking place simultaneously in New York State) while admitting that Bowie couldn't share in it. It provided a celebratory sign-off as the last track on his second LP, its long singalong coda inevitably recalling the Beatles' 'Hey Jude' of the previous year. But reviewers noted that the album still showed Bowie following tastes rather than setting them.

In September 1969, perhaps looking for emotional support after the shock of his father's death, Bowie set up home with Barnett, taking up a lease on a once-grand Victorian pile, Haddon Hall, at 42 Southend Road in Beckenham. They occupied Flat 7, on the ground floor, but over the next few months others joined them, sleeping on mattresses in the upstairs gallery, which was accessed by a grand central staircase. The house guests included Visconti and his partner Liz Hartley (who had the downstairs back bedroom), the supremely talented guitarist Mick Ronson and eventually the drummer Mick 'Woody' Woodmansey, both previously of Hull's the Rats. Bowie's half-brother Terry Burns also stayed from time to time, although his mental state had worsened following the death of his stepfather. The cellar became a rehearsal space, where songs for Bowie's third album would take shape.

During their tenure, Haddon Hall also became a locus of sexual experimentation for Bowie and Barnett. The couple wed on 19 March 1970 so that the American Angie could get a UK work permit, but kept an open marriage – although that couldn't prevent the inevitable crop of jealousies on both sides. The two often visited a gay club in Kensington known as the Sombrero, or Yours or Mine, with Angie sometimes sporting a man's short haircut and suit, and would bring back partygoers of both sexes for after-hours play. (Finnigan continued to visit Haddon Hall as a friend, not least for the Bowies' exuberant parties, but felt increasingly patronized by Angie and out of place among this new, more outré company. Eventually, she stopped coming.) During this period, too, Bowie shucked off his previous look – he's an Afghan-coated hippie with a perm in his wedding photos – for more dandified, feminine outfits, and grew his hair until it fell over his shoulders.

For Angie, Bowie wrote 'The Prettiest Star', recording it in January 1970, with Visconti producing and Marc Bolan on lead guitar. It would sink without trace, but on 22 February Bowie launched the short-lived outfit the Hype, which heralded an intriguing change of direction. When they took to the stage of Camden's Roundhouse, supporting Noel Redding's Fat Mattress, the Hype were wearing customized outfits provided by Angie; the gig was also her idea, according to Hype drummer John Cambridge. Their rock-orientated set drew heavily on numbers that would feature on Bowie's third album, alongside a cover of 'Waiting for the Man', with Bowie aping Lou Reed's acid purr. (Lindsay Kemp once described Bowie as 'a great mimic' but 'a terrible mime'.) The sound was messy, hard rock, with Ronson's amplifier over-dominant, but Bowie had thrown off the shackles of the studious singer-songwriter and moved freely, more dynamically, a frontman relishing his moment. Irked by the ironic name and dressing-up, many in the crowd literally turned their backs. But down at the front, his elbows on the stage, Bolan was watching.

The previous summer, Pitt had whisked Bowie away to a brace of songwriting contests partly because of his concern that his role as David's manager might be under threat. In fact, by now Bowie was having doubts of his own. Before the sessions for his second album, the singer had confided to Visconti that his mentor was 'too old-school' (in 2020 Visconti told *MOJO* magazine that Angie made Bowie quit Pitt). In March 1970 Bowie telephoned Philips' Olav Wyper for advice, and was put in touch with the team of the showbiz accountant Laurence Myers and with Tony Defries, the latter a lawyer in name although actually a solicitor's clerk. On the last day of March Pitt was let go, and for the next two years Myers's management company Gem Productions would cover most of Bowie's expenses.

Much of the day-to-day work of recording Bowie's third album was handled by Visconti and Ronson, who was a classically trained pianist and promising arranger as well as an outstanding guitarist (his idol was Jeff Beck). The two rigged up a basic studio underneath Haddon Hall's grand staircase, where Bowie demoed material. Despite the encouraging developments in his career, however, he preferred hanging out with his wife in a love bubble, leaving Visconti and Ronson to work up the backing tracks. 'The man would just not get out of bed and write a song,' Visconti moaned, although the resulting album would be Bowie's strongest set yet.

Meanwhile, Marc Bolan was now the pop star he'd always claimed he'd be. Released in October 1970, the Visconti-produced 'Ride a White Swan' made No. 2 in the UK. For the single, Tyrannosaurus Rex had been abbreviated to the punchier T.Rex, heralding a musical sea change: out went the folky whimsy, replaced by clean, pop-orientated directness, snippets of bright electric guitar (influenced by fifties rock 'n' rollers such as Eddie Cochran) below Bolan's distinctive warble. February 1971 gave him his first UK No. 1 in 'Hot Love', a slice of simmering sexuality that swiftly made the corkscrew-haired singer a teen pin-up. 'Get It On' (No. 1) and 'Jeepster' (No. 2) sealed the deal.

Released in the UK in April 1971 (and November 1970 in the USA), Bowie's *The Man Who Sold the World* was his strongest statement yet, its hard-rock textures backdropping tales of sci-fi apocalypse and madness. Despite its piecemeal conception, the album is a convincing, if unsettling, work, and the musicianship universally excellent. Woodmansey had replaced Cambridge, providing a sturdy core alongside Visconti on bass and Ronson's guitar. (The album's 'heavy' sound is largely down to Ronson's love of Cream.) There's no hippified optimism here – Bowie becomes a sniper in a bloodbath on 'Running Gun Blues', and envisages an all-powerful computer that solves mankind's problems but comes to despise humanity on 'Saviour Machine', while in 'The Width of a Circle' the narrator dismisses false gurus but ends up staring into the abyss of madness. (Within a year Ronson would take an extended solo on this track live – and on a cover of Cream's 'I Feel Free' – allowing Bowie to leave the stage for costume changes.) Friedrich Nietzsche's *Thus Spake Zarathustra* was a clear influence there, and in the nightmare visions of 'The Supermen', highlighting the dangers of a liberated self cut free both from God and humanity (its main riff had been given to Bowie by Jimmy Page back in 1965). Terry Burns's deteriorating mental state now saw him periodically enter Cane Hill Hospital in Coulsdon, Surrey, as a voluntary patient, and Bowie channelled his shock and frustration at his half-brother's decline into 'All the Madmen'. 'I think [Terry's] shadow is on quite a lot of the material,' he mused in 1999. 'I think I was going through an awful lot of concern about exactly what my mental condition was, and where it [might] lead.'

The album's title track went down to the wire: on the final day of mixing, Bowie still hadn't completed the lyric. But in a sign of the brilliance that he could now conjure up, he wrote it in reception at Advision Studios in Fitzrovia and recorded it immediately. An enigmatic tale of a man who meets his doppelgänger, set to a nagging riff from Ronson, it remains the LP's standout, admirably covered by Lulu on a hit in 1974 and given a gritty, understated workover 20 years later by Nirvana for their *MTV Unplugged* set.

The cover of the original UK Mercury album was testament to just how 'new' Bowie was. Draped over a chaise longue in the living room at Haddon Hall in Pre-Raphaelite languor, he wore a 'man dress' by Michael Fish (owner of the Mr Fish boutique in Mayfair) that hugged his contours right down to his leather boots. He looked like a movie starlet from Hollywood's golden age; more than one commentator has compared his appearance to that of Lauren Bacall. For the more conservative USA, an alternative cover offered a cartoon by Mike Weller of a guitar-toting cowboy; in the background stood Cane Hill. (For the LP's re-release on RCA in 1972, a third photo – a black-and-white shot of Bowie in mid-kick by Brian Ward –

was used.) Reviews were mostly upbeat; sales, less so: seven months after its US release, fewer than 1,400 copies had been bought Stateside, and in the UK the figures were even grimmer. The new single 'Holy Holy' failed to chart. Ronson and Woodmansey drifted back to Hull to re-form the Rats, initially with Visconti on bass, although he was eventually replaced by a former hairdresser named Trevor Bolder. Visconti left because he had taken a dislike to the pushy lawyer Defries, who began dropping in to Haddon Hall and joining Bowie's circle on visits to the Sombrero. But he was also irked by Bowie's perceived unprofessionalism during the album sessions – his absences with Angie and his habit of waiting until the last minute to compose melodies and lyrics. Visconti now focused on producing T.Rex instead.

Bowie wore his 'man dress' on a solo three-month promotional trip to the USA, arranged by Mercury and beginning in late January 1971, by which time Angie was five months pregnant. Having no work permit, he was able to freewheel like a tourist. In New York, Mercury press officer Ron Oberman took him to meet the street poet/composer Moondog, the epitome of an outsider artist, who made his home on the city's pavements and wore Viking costume. Bowie saw the Velvet Underground play at the Electric Circus and afterwards enthused to their curly-haired singer about the Velvets' influence on him, before discovering that he was talking not to Lou Reed, who had quit the band the previous year, but to Doug Yule. In Chicago, Oberman played him 'Paralyzed', an unhinged slice of one-chord rockabilly by the Legendary Stardust Cowboy, which Bowie immediately took to.

Bowie's jaunt to the West Coast introduced him to Rodney Bingenheimer, Mercury's radio promotions man for the region and later dubbed 'the Mayor of Sunset Strip'. At one party, Bowie fell into conversation with Bingenheimer's friend Tom Ayers, a producer for RCA. Ayers confided that the label had never really moved on from Elvis, and needed a young star for the new decade … The trip provided other pointers for Bowie's future, including his introduction to the Stooges' eponymous debut of 1969 and their follow-up *Funhouse* (1970), courtesy of John Mendelsohn, who'd been commissioned by *Rolling Stone* to interview the singer. Bowie grilled the writer about Stooges frontman Iggy Pop, while the lyrics of the band's 'TV Eye' would inform his own 'Moonage Daydream', which he penned soon after returning to the UK. The Stooges' sound was primal: incendiary rock 'n' roll topped off by Iggy's armoury of screams, drawls and – occasionally – crooning. The rock press at large treated them as a joke, but in the Stooges lay the seeds of punk and beyond. And in Iggy they had an unforgettable presence. Lithely athletic and blithely provocative on stage, he wrote spare, street-savvy lyrics perfectly attuned to teenage boredom, petulance and lustfulness. In time, Bowie's fascination with Iggy's music and persona would blossom into a genuine friendship between the two, one that endured life-threatening addictions as well as Bowie's habit of stealing ideas from anyone and everyone.

Around the same time, Bowie wrote the song that was to put him back on the path to the charts. Coming to him fully formed in January 1971, 'Oh! You Pretty Things' eventually reached No. 12 in the UK when it was covered by the ex-Herman's Hermits singer Peter Noone. His cheery rendition belied Bowie's lyrics, which describe humanity superseded by a superior race, although for Bowie this is to be welcomed – an outmoded species giving way to a more beautiful successor. He composed the song on a piano bought from a Haddon Hall neighbour, and the unfamiliar instrument drew out new compositional possibilities for him. There's an inventiveness and lightness of touch in the key changes, while the singalong chorus has an unforced simplicity. It had taken hard graft to get this far: 'I didn't know how to write a song,' he told the journalist Paul Du Noyer in 2003. 'I had no natural talents whatsoever. I made a job of work at getting good. And the only way I could learn was see how other people did it.' A week after playing the piano with Noone for 'Pretty Things' on *Top of the Pops*, Bowie was at Glastonbury, performing a dawn set that brought cold, bleary-eyed campers scurrying to the stage in delight, with 'Memory of a Free Festival' ringing out as the sun rose.

Duncan Zowie Haywood Jones was born on 30 May 1971. He was a hefty baby, weighing in at nearly 4 kg, and Angie cracked her pelvis during the painful birth. Afterwards she went on holiday to Italy with Bowie's former girlfriend Dana Gillespie to recuperate. The Bowies swiftly hired a nanny, Sue Frost, to look after Zowie (an approximation of the Greek female name Zoë, meaning 'life'). Bowie celebrated his son's birth with the charming 'Kooks'. The song made its public debut on a BBC *In Concert* programme four days later, for which Ronson was coaxed down from Hull along with Woodmansey and Bolder, who'd been playing together in the band Ronno.

To co-produce his next album, *Hunky Dory*, Bowie enrolled Ken Scott, who'd been an engineer on George Harrison's magnum opus *All Things Must Pass* the year before. Scott was astounded at the quality of Bowie's material – the expansiveness of its melodies, the octave swoops and odd diversions. 'Space Oddity' keyboardist Rick Wakeman was recalled, and his piano parts form the core of the LP's songs, played on a Bechstein grand that had graced the Beatles' 'Hey Jude'. '[Bowie] wanted the album to be very piano-orientated,' Wakeman told the *Guardian* in 2017. 'I was given complete freedom.' The two men gelled, and Bowie subsequently even asked if Wakeman would join his backing band. On the same day, though, Wakeman had the same offer from Yes. Bowie was gracious in defeat.

Kicking off with the chord changes from Eddie Cochran's 'Three Steps to Heaven', 'Queen Bitch' paid vibrant homage to the Velvets in Bowie's almost-spoken narration and the theme of gay street life, although its thrilling Ronson-led drive is atypical of the rest of the album. Instead, piano dominates, from the deceptively playful 'Oh! You Pretty Things' to the magisterial 'Life on Mars?!', whose intoxicatingly abstruse lyrics are paired with chords that cheekily nod to 'My Way'. (Kenneth Pitt had tried to get Bowie the gig of writing English lyrics to the French original, 'Comme d'Habitude'; Paul Anka won out.) 'Changes' is the definitive Bowie statement, encapsulating the drive to push ahead and the generations left behind, while 'The Bewlay Brothers' provides a bittersweet sign-off. Each song is housed in its own setting, utterly true to itself – a tribute to Ronson's skilful arrangements, although he'd fretted that he wasn't up to the job.

For the cover shoot, Bowie brought along a book about Marlene Dietrich as inspiration for the photographer, Brian Ward. The results were hand-coloured by Terry Pastor, rendering Bowie a timeless androgyne gazing wistfully into the distance. On its release, *Hunky Dory* garnered unqualified praise. *NME*'s Danny Holloway saw it as possibly the most vital release by an up-and-coming artist in 1972, 'because he's not following trends – he's setting them'. *Rock* magazine predicted that 'He has the genius to be to the 70s what Lennon, McCartney, Jagger and Dylan were to the 60s.' That chimed neatly with Defries's statement of intent to Bowie's new label, RCA: 'You've had nothing since the 1950s, and you missed out on the sixties. But you can own the 1970s. Because David Bowie is going to remake the decade, just like the Beatles did in the 1960s.'

4

Rock 'n' Roll Alien

For all his stylistic about-turns in the sixties and his development into a songwriter of distinction by the time of *Hunky Dory*, David Bowie's nebulous talents didn't truly coalesce into one singular vision until his creation of Ziggy Stardust. Ziggy would look like no rock star ever before, an image newly crafted for the still-young seventies. A beautiful but unnerving creature with a wardrobe straight out of a space opera, Ziggy was a piece of rock 'n' roll alchemy, although the base elements from which he arose had been around for some time. They ranged from the science-fiction novels that Bowie had loved for years to the messianic madness of Vince Taylor. Little Richard's pizzazz and ambivalent sexuality were somewhere in the mix, along with a smattering of Eddie Cochran's chugging riffs and Judy Garland's heart-lifting optimism in *The Wizard of Oz*. In presenting Ziggy on stage, Bowie would incorporate mime skills he'd learned from Lindsay Kemp, while his out-there costumes were inspired by the glitz and glamour he had soaked up from Kemp's crowd and at the Sombrero. The name had come to him in February 1971, inspired by the Legendary Stardust Cowboy and by Iggy Pop.

In September 1971 Bowie's entourage, including Angie and Tony Defries, made a brief but remarkably eventful trip to New York to sign a three-album contract with RCA, a deal brokered by Laurence Myers. Staking their claim to future fame, they stayed in the penthouse suite at the Warwick Hotel, where the Beatles usually lodged during their visits to the city in the mid-sixties. Bowie finally met Iggy himself at Max's Kansas City on Park Avenue South. He and Defries were enchanted. Later events soured Iggy's impressions of both men, but at that point in his career they offered him a lifeline: for all his talent, feral stagecraft and charisma, Iggy was a down-on-his-luck heroin addict. Defries signed him to Gem and in due course arranged a new recording contract for him at CBS/Columbia.

Earlier that evening Bowie had finally got to meet the real Lou Reed, dining with New York's revered and some-what feared street poet and his wife, Bettye. Bowie also met Andy Warhol at the Factory, although it proved an awkward meeting. In his caprice, unapologetic artifice and conscious manufacture of a public persona, the artist had been an important early inspiration to Bowie, who had written *Hunky Dory*'s 'Andy Warhol' as, in his own words, 'an ironic *hommage*'. But when he played him an acetate of the recording, the King of Pop Art left the room. He cared even less for an impromptu mime that the singer performed, in which he pretended to disembowel himself. He did like Bowie's shoes, though, which had been given to him by Marc Bolan. 'Brilliant canary yellow, semi-wedge heel, semi-point rounded toe,' Bowie recalled.

Back in the UK, a nervous Bowie debuted a selection of songs from his next album with a powerhouse trio of Mick Ronson, bassist Trevor Bolder and drummer Woody

Woodmansey on 25 September at Friars Aylesbury (also known as the Friars Club at the Borough Assembly Hall), a convivial venue for trying out new material. With Bowie still wearing long locks and his Mr Fish man dress, the band impressed – Friars' manager David Stopps thought Bowie 'fantastic' – but thereafter he and the band ensconced themselves in Underhill Studio, Greenwich, honing the material further before their next live gigs, some four months later. As RCA prepared to release *Hunky Dory*, Bowie and his band were already recording its follow-up in Trident Studios, the singer still sporting his Pre-Raphaelite tresses.

Songs were only part of it. The look was crucial, too, and marked out Bowie-as-Ziggy even from fellow travellers such as Bolan and Roxy Music, whose make-up, glitter and shiny tat meant they would all be grouped together at the time as 'glam rock'. At Angie's suggestion, Bolder employed his hairdressing skills to crop Bowie's long hair, instantly distancing him from the previous generation's peace-and-love brigade. 'You have to try and kill your elders,' he maintained in 2002. 'We had to develop a completely new vocabulary ... To take the recent past and restructure it in a way that we felt we had authorship of ... that was our world, not the bloody hippie thing.' The writer William Gibson sensed as much. Passing through London in the early seventies, he picked up on glam as an inter-generational line in the sand: 'I remember thinking that it was the first time I'd ever seen anything that felt truly post-Sixties,' he told the *New Statesman* in 2020. 'This is not my thing, this is for slightly younger people.' Bowie would have bristled at being lumped together with the likes of the Sweet, though, whom he regarded as chancers still shackled to rock's heritage. In radical contrast, he was incorporating elements from outside that tradition: Expressionist cinema, kabuki, contemporary mime and theatre, Dada. He described himself and his more ambitious peers (Roxy again) as 'avant-garde explorers' and – in a term even he admitted was snobbish – 'high glam'.

Bowie worked with Freddie Burretti, a talented fashion singer and Sombrero regular, on Ziggy's various outfits, drawing heavily on the boiler suits of Alex and his droogs in Stanley Kubrick's controversial movie *A Clockwork Orange*. They gleaned ideas from pre-release stills taken from the film, which would not be released in the UK until 13 January 1972. Bowie credited Kubrick with more than just costume inspiration, though: 'For me and several of my friends, the seventies were the start of the twenty-first century. It was Kubrick's doing, on the whole, with *2001* and *A Clockwork Orange* … there was a distinct feeling that "nothing was true" any more and that the future was not as clear-cut as it seemed.' (In *Who's a Dandy?* [2002], George Walden lists several 'key attributes of dandyism – the detachment, the irony, the impertinence, the nihilism, the provocation' – all of which fitted Ziggy Stardust like a skintight bodysuit.) The lyrics of several songs on the forthcoming album nodded to the Nadsat lingo that Anthony Burgess had devised for the original novel. The sweeping optimism of Beethoven's 'Ode to Joy', interpreted on synthesizer by Walter Carlos for the movie's soundtrack, would announce Ziggy's stage entrance. Intriguingly (given how Bowie's path was to criss-cross with that of Mick Jagger in the seventies), before Kubrick bought the rights to *A Clockwork Orange* the photographer

Michael Cooper and writer Terry Southern were working on a treatment of Burgess's novel that envisaged Jagger as its protagonist, Alex. The rest of the Rolling Stones were to play his droog henchmen.

An interview with *Melody Maker*'s Michael Watts, published on 22 January 1972, provided Ziggy with a dazzling launch pad. Although Bowie's sexual activities were not restricted to women, many observers felt that he'd regarded dalliances with men as experimental one-offs. No matter: 'I'm gay and always have been, even when I was David Jones,' he claimed, a bold statement at a time when homosexuality was still treated with suspicion if not outright contempt. Watts observed that he frequently dropped in words from Polari – slang still used by the British gay community at the time. Reading through it, you can hear Bowie starting to grow into the role he'll play. He's coy and camp, revelling in the moment and utterly confident. As much as anything, the piece is a terrific 'fuck you', unfurling the flag for outsiders everywhere. Be what you want to be, he seems to be saying. Invent yourself. And again, he's closing the curtain on the previous decade. 'Would you Let Your Sister Go With a Rolling Stone?', screamed one provocative *Melody Maker* headline in 1964. Come 1972, would you let your brother hang out with David Bowie?

On 31 March 1972 Bowie signed a contract with Defries's new management company, MainMan. Defries's drive and belief, like Angie's, would be crucial to Bowie's breakthrough. 'Without their constant support and input, there would never have been a Ziggy, or an Aladdin, or a future Bowie for that matter,' maintains Tony Visconti. But although he didn't realize it at the time, the singer's contract designated him as an employee – rather than partner – in MainMan, something that would come back to haunt him.

Ziggy Stardust and the Spiders from Mars brought their message to the masses on a tour of the UK from late January to May 1972, warming up with a return to Friars Aylesbury. The venue was crowded and the set a scorcher. The tour proper kicked off at the Toby Jug, a small pub in Tolworth, Surrey. By the time they played Manchester's Free Trade Hall on 21 April, Ziggy was able to step out into the audience, supported by the upturned hands of the fans, á la Iggy at the Cincinnati Pop Festival two years earlier. And on 27 June, at Oxford Town Hall, he sank towards the stage between Ronson's legs, his teeth grazing the guitarist's upraised Les Paul in a fellatio-like gesture, a moment immortalized by photographer Mick Rock. Pete Townshend had smashed guitars; Jimi Hendrix burned them; David Bowie went down on them.

Released on 6 June, *The Rise and Fall of Ziggy Stardust and the Spiders from Mars* elicited warm praise. 'His bid for stardom is accelerating at lightning speed,' Watts gushed in *Melody Maker*; while *NME*'s James Johnson dubbed him 'our most futuristic songwriter'. For the album's sleeve, Bowie posed for Brian Ward outside the photographer's studio on Heddon Street, just off Regent Street, sporting a quilted jumpsuit he'd designed with Burretti. (With neat synchronicity, the shoot took place on the day of *A Clockwork Orange*'s UK release.) Terry Pastor was again called in to colour the sleeve, adding to the images an ambience that seemed to hint simultaneously at the past – a whiff of forties noir – and at a tantalizing future, a Janus-like state mirrored in the music itself.

It gives the impression of being a concept album of sorts, with a narrative arc where none had been intended; Bowie later commented that he'd planned it as a musical but hadn't had the time to finish it. Even so, it's a distinctively left-field story. Ziggy the rock 'n' roll extraterrestrial messiah arrives from the stars to announce Earth's imminent apocalypse. The opener, 'Five Years', is a poetic farewell to a dying planet, the narrative a whirl of memories and snapshots, with even strangers suddenly of inestimable value. Ziggy becomes a star and saviour of the world but burns out in the process ('Hang on to Yourself', 'Ziggy Stardust'). As the stage fades to black, 'Rock 'n' Roll Suicide' provides the coda, a burned-out star facing his demise in a song that builds from guitar arpeggios dialled in from the fifties to a euphoric swell of strings and emotion. Gloriously melodramatic, a grand finale par excellence, it offers open arms to misfits and lost tribes everywhere. 'It Ain't Easy' and the thundering 'Suffragette City' don't fit particularly neatly into that scenario, so it's perhaps a tribute to the album's sequencing that the listener senses there might be a coherent story in there somewhere. Step back, though, see the broader strokes and it makes greater sense as a parable of the ecstatic rush of fame and the price it exacts.

RCA's Dennis Katz loved it, but he didn't hear a single. In response, Bowie penned 'Starman', mixing rose-tinted familiarity (the rise of an octave at the start of its chorus is a nod to Judy Garland's 'Over the Rainbow') with the prospect of a rock 'n' roll alien connecting with the kids over the radio. Woodmansey credits it as the song that ultimately won over the crowd at concerts: 'Initially, audiences did not like that show. The front few rows would be giving us V-signs … It was only when "Starman" got all over the radio that things turned.'

The song, which would return Bowie to the UK Top 10, made its television debut on 21 June, on ITV's *Lift Off with Ayshea*. But its airing on 6 July on BBC's half-hour *Top of the Pops* – by then an institution for young British music fans – was something else altogether. The sight of Bowie cosying up to Ronson at the mike stand and languorously draping an arm around his guitarist's shoulders – his fingernails daubed in white nail varnish – was not standard fare for post-teatime TV. Ditto the moment when Bowie sang 'you', looking straight down the camera and twirling his finger playfully at millions of viewers. But his appearance alone could have done the trick: clad in a figure-hugging, multi-coloured costume designed by Burretti, his hair spruced into a spiky mullet. Mismatched eyes; smirking lips.

Perhaps its impact has been overstated; did the playgrounds of Great Britain truly buzz with disbelief the next day? Certainly, plenty of later pop giants cite Bowie's performance that night as a game-changer. Ian McCulloch of Echo and the Bunnymen recalled seeing it as a 12-year-old: 'It was rare to see that kind of flamboyance … It was like "Bloody hell". The presence of it.' Gary Kemp of new romantic pin-ups Spandau Ballet saw it as 'My seminal moment … [it] set my benchmark for how pop music should look. It had to be visual.' Of the many accounts of its transformative effect, perhaps the neatest is that of the inspirational Creation Records boss Alan McGee. 'The reason I got into rock 'n' roll,' he said, 'is because I saw David Bowie on *Top of the Pops* playing "Starman".'

* * * * *

Sessions for *Ziggy Stardust* had dovetailed with those for *Hunky Dory*. 'The two albums almost melded into one thing for us, at the time,' noted the producer Ken Scott in 2003. '"It Ain't Easy" was recorded for one, ended up on the other.' What distinguishes the later album most clearly from its predecessor is Bowie's use of Ziggy as a mask through which he could speak in character, bringing theatre into rock music in a way that had never been attempted so comprehensively. True, this conceit came to the project late in the day, but the idea of slipping into another persona would serve him well.

As Bowie's star was rising, that of another act appeared to have sputtered out. Mott the Hoople were a formidable live act of the late sixties, but remained hitless after four albums, fed up with thankless touring and depressed by an unpromising contract with Island Records. Bowie had heard and liked their albums *Wildlife* and *Brain Capers*; perhaps he'd even seen them live. Certainly, as with Iggy and the Stooges, there was an intrinsic rock 'n' roll effervescence to Mott that Bowie, always the most intellectual and controlled of pop stars, couldn't quite reproduce. In March, hearing that Mott were on the point of breaking up, he had offered them the as-yet-unreleased 'Suffragette City' as a potential hit single and a way to stave off the split. Remarkably, they turned it down, whereupon Bowie put forward another song, so new that he hadn't quite finished it: 'All the Young Dudes'. He played it to them sitting cross-legged on the floor at Gem's Regent Street offices. 'Everyone in Mott knew right away that it was a hit,' the lead singer, Ian Hunter, marvelled. 'I would never have given that song away to anybody.'

Interviewed with the Beat writer William Burroughs in February 1974 for *Rolling Stone*, Bowie insisted the song was in the same vein as 'Five Years', a picture of a doomed planet running out of natural resources, a Kubrickian dystopia with a finite lifespan. (Another rejection of sixties mores: the faith in collectively building a progressively better world superseded by the fear that the Earth's future is troubled and all too brief.) 'The older people have lost all touch with reality and the kids are left on their own to plunder anything,' Bowie informed Burroughs. With no electricity for broadcasts, 'Ziggy's adviser tells him to collect news and sing it ... So Ziggy does this and there is terrible news. "All the Young Dudes" is a song about this news.' Well, he should know – but who picked up on that at the time? Heard without the trappings of its conceptual background, the lyrics seem more pertinent as a wedge between glam and the fuzzy philosophies of the late sixties, perhaps even an implicit celebration of gay love. Rightly or wrongly, it made far more sense as a generational anthem, one that took Mott to No. 3 in the UK charts in September that year, higher than Bowie himself had charted so far.

In July Lou Reed joined Bowie and the Spiders at the Royal Festival Hall in London on the Velvets' euphoric 'Sweet Jane' and 'White Light/White Heat'; Reed and Iggy famously flanked Bowie at a press conference at the Dorchester Hotel for another iconic photo by Mick Rock. By August Bowie was co-producing Reed's next album with Ronson, and Scott serving as engineer; *Transformer* would recharge Reed's batteries at a time when drug addiction had sent his career off the tracks. Bowie's tasks involved tackling Reed's mood swings as well overseeing the music. (In April 1979 the two were reunited at one of Reed's London gigs and later had dinner at a Chelsea restaurant. But soon Reed was slapping Bowie and screaming 'Don't you *ever* say that to me!' He'd asked Bowie to produce his next album. Bowie replied that he'd do it only if Reed cleaned up.)

By now, Suzi Fussey (Bowie's mum's hairdresser and Mick Ronson's future wife) had refined Bowie's already startling hairstyle, back-combing the top, trimming the sides and dyeing the whole thing a vibrant red. Angie was again a key instigator, although according to Bowie himself the inspiration had been a magazine photoshoot for Japanese fashion designer Kansai Yamamoto, whose models wore a red kabuki lion's wig. Yamamoto would have a continuing influence on Bowie's changing appearance; his future contributions – seen on Bowie's tour the following year – included an asymmetric knitted bodysuit, a cape bearing Japanese *kanji* script, and a remarkable vinyl bodysuit dubbed 'Tokyo Pop', featuring a pair of voluminous semicircles for legs.

In a sign of Bowie's burgeoning popularity, the front door of Haddon Hall was now regularly besieged by fans, among them future pop luminary George O'Dowd – Boy George. The Bowies were forced to move, first to a flat in Vale Court, a mansion block in Maida Vale, sublet by *Avengers* star Diana Rigg. She evicted them because of their noisiness, and they eventually settled in a five-floor house in Oakley Street, off the King's Road in Chelsea, just around the corner from Mick and Bianca Jagger in Cheyne Walk. Reportedly, in its sitting room they created 'The Pit', a fur-covered bed where guests indulged in orgies while those too shy or too tired to participate simply watched.

For two gigs at the Rainbow theatre in Finsbury Park on 19 and 20 August 1972, Bowie unveiled an ambitious multimedia experience, incorporating dramatic lighting and sets. Lindsay Kemp and his mime troupe performed on a gangway above the stage. At one point, Bowie dropped the opening line of 'Over the Rainbow' into 'Starman', a wry rebuff to those critics who'd yet to succumb to Ziggymania. Its parent album peaked at No. 5 in the UK and would remain in the charts for two years. In its wake, *Hunky Dory* charted for the first time, making No. 3 and staying there for more than a year. Even the brooding *The Man Who Sold the World* became a Top 30 hit. By the end of the following year, David Bowie would be Britain's bestselling rock star.

But the UK alone was never enough. For true stardom, Bowie and Defries had always known that they'd have to break America. And it was there that their focus now shifted.

5

'Ziggy Goes to America'

The seeds of Ziggy's demise were sown on the US tour that began in Cleveland on 22 September 1972 and finished, aside from a brief return to the UK, on 12 March 1973 at the Hollywood Palladium in Los Angeles. Angie and David crossed to America in style on the *QE2*. (Bowie was terrified of air travel at the time, triggered by a traumatic flight through an electrical storm on the way back from a break in Cyprus in July.) At the RCA studios in New York they auditioned pianists for the tour, quickly settling on the avant-jazz keyboardist Mike Garson after he'd improvised over just a few bars of 'Changes'.

The East Coast audiences readily took Ziggy to their hearts – Cleveland was a huge success, and Philadelphia and New York followed suit – as did most of the West Coast. But the rest of the tour was patchy. Many Americans, if they'd even heard of Bowie, didn't know what to make of this skinny, pasty-faced androgyne, and the size of the States meant that he couldn't make his impact as immediately and vividly as he had in the UK. That meant shows in arenas less than a quarter full, or outright cancellations. More positively, Bowie was becoming an increasingly assured performer, as can be heard on a recording of a gig at Santa Monica Civic Auditorium on 20–21 October 1972. Widely bootlegged until its official release in 2008, it captures the band at their live peak. 'I can tell that I'm totally into being Ziggy by this stage of our touring,' Bowie reflected. 'It's no longer an act; I am him.'

In his essay 'The Decay of Lying', Oscar Wilde wrote that 'Life imitates Art far more than Art imitates Life', an aphorism that Bowie was living out in 1972 and 1973. That carried attendant risks, of course. Elvis Presley – whom Bowie saw in concert at Madison Square Garden earlier that year– could have told him as much. In a candid moment during a press conference before the shows in June, Elvis admitted: 'The image is one thing and a human being is another … It's very hard to live up to an image.'

For a British pop lover who'd grown up on a diet of US-minted rock 'n' roll, jazz and the Beats, touring the States threw up plentiful nuggets of inspiration for songwriting. New single 'The Jean Genie' was worked up on the Greyhound tour bus and recorded at RCA's New York studios in October; released in November, it would make No. 2 in the UK, Bowie's highest chart placing to date. Its inspiration was probably the Yardbirds' 1965 cover of 'I'm a Man', with its wailing harmonica and trademark 'rave-up' section. But its main riff had a storied past: Bo Diddley's original of 1955 was adapted by Muddy Waters for 'Manish Boy' (the inspiration for the name of Bowie's sixties R&B band) of the same year. Diddley's 'I'm a Man' had itself borrowed from 'I'm Your Hoochie-Coochie Man', written by Willie Dixon and recorded by Waters in 1954. And if you'd tuned in to *Top of the Pops* on 11 January 1973, you'd have heard that riff *twice*: in 'The Jean Genie', played over shots of the crowd dancing, and in the Sweet's No. 1 'Blockbuster'.

The title nodded (probably subconsciously) to Jean Genet, one of Kemp's favourite writers, but the personification in song owed far more to Bowie's impressions of Iggy Pop – 'a white-trash kind of trailer-park kid ... the closet intellectual who wouldn't want the world to know that he reads,' as he mused later. After the Santa Monica gigs, Bowie took time off and devoted himself to mixing the bulk of Iggy and the Stooges' next album in one day at Western Sound Recorders in Los Angeles. Released as *Raw Power* in February 1973, it became a blueprint for countless punk bands – Sex Pistol Steve Jones claimed to have learned guitar while playing along to it on speed. Bowie's mix came in for much criticism, not least from the Stooges themselves, who thought it was weighted too heavily towards guitar and vocals at the expense of bass, although a mix by Iggy himself in the nineties also had its detractors.

Defries's strategy was to break Bowie as a star, not a star in the making. In this he was one with Bowie himself, who had long practised what we'd now term 'positive visualization'. Woodmansey recalled that at their first meeting, before working on *The Man Who Sold the World*, 'He was assuming he'd made it already,' while the photographer Mick Rock noted that when Bowie played live in the early Ziggy days, 'It was as though he was playing to a much bigger audience.' But it went back far further: 'When he joined The Kon-Rads I could tell that he was determined,' George Underwood recalled. 'I think he almost dreamed it before he did it. Everything he did had roots back to the sixties.'

MainMan's entourage was booked into the best hotels, all expenses paid, with RCA subsidizing – for now, anyway.

(Simon Napier-Bell estimated that it cost the label $400,000 at the time – millions today.) The band, as they'd discover to their horror, were being paid only statutory Musician's Union rates. There were personal problems, too, as Angie's on-tour shenanigans (including flings with two Stooges, bassist Ron Asheton and guitarist James Williamson, as well as Iggy's friend Scott Richardson from Detroit) raised eyebrows. Drugs – mainly Quaaludes (methaqualone) – were becoming a problem, although towards the end of the tour cocaine, by then ubiquitous in the US music industry, had made inroads into Bowie's circle. When the tour hit Los Angeles in October, the entourage were greeted with an array of narcotic and carnal temptations, some courtesy of Rodney Bingenheimer, while Bowie's sexual appetite during this period is a matter of record – 'rooting himself silly', in Ronson's words. Both Angie and MainMan publicist Cherry Vanilla have suggested that Bowie was addicted to sex at the time, while Richardson remembered 'waking up under a pile of bodies' at Haddon Hall, where he lived for a while.

The plentiful sex may have played its part in Bowie's increasing disengagement from Angie, who could be a turbulent and disruptive presence, possibly because her own chances at stardom had been so comprehensively obscured by the spotlight on him. Aside from the one-night stands, he'd keep a number of longer-term girlfriends. For her part, Angie enjoyed trysts with, among others, Mickey Finn, the percussionist with Marc Bolan's T.Rex, which must have been uniquely irksome for Bowie. As the tour wore on, Angie's behaviour began to exasperate both him and his management, and after a night-time frolic in a hotel pool with one lover, she was sent packing. She would never tour full-time with him again. Something of all that decadent indulgence fed into 'Cracked Actor', written for Bowie's next album. An explicit narrative of a Hollywood star gone to seed, coldly directing his paid lovers in how to pleasure him, it was written in the light of four hedonistic days at the Beverly Hills Hotel.

A brief return to the UK for Christmas 1972 saw two more back-to-back gigs at the Rainbow, during which collections were made for Bowie's father's charity, Barnardo's. Either side of the festive season, the finishing touches were made to Bowie's sixth album, *Aladdin Sane*. Recorded partly in the USA, but mostly in London's Trident Studios in a rush before Ziggy and the Spiders' return to the States, it had amassed pre-orders of 100,000 in the UK, making it the bestselling LP in the UK since the Beatles, a major symbolic coup. It shot straight to No. 1 and took up residence there for five weeks, dropping off the charts only after nearly 18 months. The template of *Ziggy* remained, but overlaid with a host of new elements – notably Garson, whose playing gives the album its singular character, as Rick Wakeman's had on *Hunky Dory*. Garson adds a whiff of twenties stride piano and Weimar-era Germany to the lurch and bounce of 'Time', while his dappled runs on 'Lady Grinning Soul' – 'French with a little Franz Liszt thrown in there', according to the pianist himself – turns a beautiful track into something transcendent. His work on the title track is the standout, though: early bright ripples and punctuating chords give way to a minute-and-a-half solo of exploratory jazz, a free-form riot that seems to orbit the song rather than be anchored to it.

Elsewhere, Ronson's raw guitar and fearsome riffs dominate. The glam-stomp of 'Panic in Detroit' soundtracks the city's precipitous decline. ('I thought, I wonder if Kubrick has seen this town,' Bowie recalled. 'It makes his kind of world in *Clockwork Orange* look kind of pansy!') Concerned that *Ziggy Stardust* had been too polished, Bowie wanted a rougher sound this time, and the Rolling Stones, in particular Jagger, are an audible influence. He quipped that he'd written the R&B-influenced 'The Jean Genie' to piss Jagger off (his harmonica-playing certainly recalls that of Jagger on the Stones' debut LP), but paid tribute too with a helter-skelter take on 'Let's Spend the Night Together' by name-dropping the singer in 'Drive-in Saturday', and by injecting 'Watch That Man' with a groove straight off the Stones' album *Exile on Main St* of the previous year. But Bowie's fascination with the Stones went way back; they'd been in the vanguard of the blues and R&B explosion that the young David Jones had adored, and strived so hard to join in the mid-sixties. Moreover, Jagger was an object lesson in how to transcend your prosaic roots – in his case, a middle-class upbringing in Dartford – by dreaming up a vibrant alter ego (blues-bawling rebel sex god) and faking it so wholeheartedly that it becomes true.

In the seventies, Bowie's record sleeves were a gallery for each new musical identity, but *Aladdin Sane*, shot by the fashion photographer Brian Duffy, has enjoyed the longest afterlife. Broadly, he's still Ziggy, save for the jagged red-and-blue flash that runs from hairline to jawline. Duffy had spotted the motif on a Panasonic kettle, but it had more intriguing connotations too, including the Taking Care of Business (TCB) thunderbolt adopted by Elvis Presley. It may allude to a split personality, since his half-brother Terry was still very much on Bowie's mind. And, whether intentionally or not, it had fascistic implications. Reviewing Bowie's gig on 2 July 1973 at Hammersmith Odeon for the *New Statesman*, Martin Amis commented on the stage's 'SS lightning flashes'.

Largely written during, and informed by, Bowie's exhausting US jaunt, *Aladdin Sane* rivals its predecessor for brilliance, although inconsistency and an unhinged quality to some of the tracks hint at the strain its composer was now under. By the time he finally took a break, in mid-1973, he had been touring for a year and a half. 'It was all too obvious that the heat was on,' reflected Charles Shaar Murray. 'The songs were written too fast, recorded too fast and mixed too fast.' The album's itinerant creation is acknowledged in the song titles, which include bracketed references to where they were written. But in retrospect, all this makes the set even more authentic as a memento of Bowie's US tour and the frantic trajectory he was now on.

* * * * *

He resumed touring in the USA on 14 February 1973, beginning at the celebrated Radio City Music Hall in New York; even Salvador Dalí turned up. But things gradually began to unravel. Bowie seldom socialized with his band, save for post-show parties. And despite his reassurance, they were now openly complaining about their pay – especially after Garson unwittingly revealed that he was earning $800 per week; Woodmansey and Bolder were on $50. Defries side-lined Ronson, promising him a solo deal and further dividing the band. (And anyway, it didn't work out for Ronson, who was a superb guitarist and arranger but no frontman.)

April found Bowie sailing from San Francisco to Yokohama on the SS *Oronsay* to play nine dates in Japan that transformed him from a little-known cult into a phenomenon. By now he had become a supremely confident and original performer, delivering his singalong songs about alienation and apocalypse, sex and rock 'n' roll suicide while dressed in improbable costumes by Yamamoto that were works of art in themselves. In a brief thawing of relations, Angie was invited over; backstage at gigs, Zowie played games with Yamamoto's young daughter. Afterwards, Bowie and his old friend Geoffrey MacCormack (a backing singer on the tour) travelled back to the UK in style on the Trans-Siberian Express.

Meanwhile, Bowie's golden touch for other artists struck again: Lou Reed's *Transformer* had yielded a surprise transatlantic hit in the soft-shoe sleaze of 'Walk on the Wild Side' (UK No. 10/US No. 16), packed with portraits of Warholian 'superstars' from the Factory. Its parent album made UK No. 13 and hit the Top 30 Stateside. With songs of the quality of 'Vicious', 'Satellite of Love' and 'Perfect Day', and the cachet of Bowie as producer, *Transformer* gave Reed his career bestseller, although many hardened Velvet Underground fans felt his sound had been tamed, and blamed Bowie for it. Iggy Pop was less fortunate; boredom brought on by Defries losing focus, or interest, in them had caused the Stooges to binge on drugs and sex in their MainMan-financed Hollywood mansion. They were thrown out and dropped by Defries's company, and Iggy was directionless again.

RCA had underwritten the huge losses from Bowie's first US jaunt, but now zipped up the wallet. It occurred to Defries that by taking Bowie out of the picture for a while, he could not only give his artist a break, and build up expectation for his return, but also wouldn't have to finance the next planned American tour himself. Some people knew what was afoot – Fussey (now the star's personal hairdresser and PA), Ronson, the roadies – but were sworn to secrecy. Woodmansey and Bolder had no idea what was coming at the finale of their gig on 3 July at Hammersmith Odeon. The show was a blinder, with Jeff Beck joining them on-stage and Ronson playing out of his skin. But just before the last song, Bowie approached the microphone and calmed the crowd. 'This show will stay the longest in our memories,' he began cryptically. 'Not just because it is the end of the tour but because it is the last show we'll ever do.' A moment's silence was followed by confused screams of disbelief. Then Ronson picked out the opening to 'Rock 'n' Roll Suicide'. And with that, the Spiders' days were over.

The following night, at a star-studded end-of-tour party at the Café Royal, Bowie hobnobbed with the likes of Mick and Bianca Jagger, Paul and Linda McCartney, Lou Reed, Tony Curtis, Lulu (whom he'd met in Sheffield towards the end of the UK tour) and Barbra Streisand. The 'retirement' was intended to apply only to the character of Ziggy Stardust, although many at Hammersmith Odeon that night would have assumed that Bowie himself was quitting the music business. Bolder was too mortified by his abrupt sacking to attend the party, but Woodmansey did show up. The drummer was never to return to Bowie's circle, but Bolder was retained for his next album, which was already in the pipeline. It would be a place-holder, to keep his music out there while he built up the energy and ideas for another audacious project.

Bowie regularly featured cover versions on his albums, perhaps to test himself against greatness, perhaps as an *hommage* to an artist he admired. His seventh album, *Pin Ups* (1976), would be devoted entirely to them, focusing on the mod anthems and R&B that he'd adored. (The cover pairs him with sixties supermodel Twiggy, whom he'd name-checked in 'Drive-in Saturday'.) Recorded at the Château d'Hérouville outside Paris, the album actually outperformed its predecessor at the time, with 150,000 advance orders. Writing in *Melody Maker*, Michael Watts noted perceptively that 'it affords him the chance of his favourite pastime: role-playing', but overall *Pin Ups* feels unconvincing and a lesser work. The best of the bunch, a cover of the Merseys' 1966 hit 'Sorrow', itself a cover of the McCoys' original, was a worthy UK No. 3; its B-side was his take on Jacques Brel's 'Amsterdam'. Bowie had seen the Syd Barrett-era Pink Floyd at the Marquee and UFO back in the day, and the psychedelic prince had left an indelible impression on him. 'Along with Anthony Newley, he was the first guy I'd heard to sing pop or rock with a British accent,' Bowie said years later, after Barrett's death. 'His impact on my thinking was enormous.' But his *Pin Ups* take on the Floyd's hit 'See Emily Play' from 1967 lacks spark.

Still, Bowie's stellar success was acknowledged by RCA at the end of the year, in the form of a plaque celebrating his placing five albums in the UK charts simultaneously. Breaking America remained the goal. (He would move to the States in April 1974, first settling in Manhattan's Chelsea district.) For the US broadcaster NBC, he made *The 1980 Floor Show* in October 1973, a series of performances of recent tracks, accompanied by mime and dance. In keeping with the retrospective theme of his previous album, it was filmed in the Marquee, and Marianne Faithfull – another of the sixties defining faces – joined him to duet on Sonny and Cher's 'I Got You Babe'. Faithfull dressed as a nun for the occasion; when she turned around, a gap in her robe exposed her buttocks.

During the sessions for *Pin Ups*, Bowie also took the time to record covers of 'The Man Who Sold the World' and 'Watch that Man' with Lulu. He played sax on her hit version of the former, which he produced with Ronson. Promoting the single, Lulu cross-dressed to the nines in a suit and trilby, perhaps reminding some in Bowie's circle of Angie at the Sombrero, or possibly even the gender-bending clubbers of Weimar-era Berlin.

6

Diamond Dogs
and the Thin White Duke

With *Diamond Dogs* (1974), Bowie maintained the uncompromising attitude that had characterized every original album since *The Man Who Sold the World*. Inspired largely by his thwarted ambitions for a musical based on George Orwell's *Nineteen Eighty-Four* (the writer's widow, Sonia, turned Bowie down flat), the album proffers a hellish vision of the future: Hunger City, inspired partly by *Metropolis*, Fritz Lang's landmark sci-fi movie of 1927. Roller-skating gangs hunt the dark streets, Dickensian thieves crossed with *A Clockwork Orange*'s droogs and decked out in looted jewellery – hence 'Diamond Dogs'.

Atypical of its bleak parent album, the single 'Rebel Rebel' features another memorable riff, largely by Bowie himself, who plays much of the guitar on the set. With its 'Satisfaction'-like beat, it underlines his continuing fascination with, and determination to out-do, Mick Jagger. (Tellingly, *Melody Maker*'s review of *Hunky Dory* had called him 'Mick Jagger's heir'.) A swansong for his glam-rock sound, it gave him a UK No. 5 hit, but stalled at No. 64 on *Billboard*, indicative of how low his stock remained Stateside. The album's title track only scraped to No. 21 in the UK;

an odder and bleaker prospect, it opens with a delirious crowd and Bowie talking genocide and name-checking Halloween Jack, his new alter ego.

Diamond Dogs illustrates how comprehensively Bowie had now surpassed his friend Marc Bolan. Whereas T.Rex seemed stuck in a glam rut, Bowie was pushing on into new, stranger territory, unconcerned that it might alienate his fans. In his previous three albums, his songs had been narratives that listeners could follow. For *Diamond Dogs*, however, he employed 'cut-ups', as famously practised by the writers Brion Gysin and William Burroughs, to construct the album's disjointed and disconcerting lyrics, snipping out individual lines or words from a text and reassembling them to provide a new narrative. Burroughs's stories of deviancy, decadence and addiction are a palpable influence on the overall atmosphere too. The howl that opens the album sets the tone, while a spoken-word intro to 'Future Legend' maps out the desolate prospects. The ghost of Bowie's aborted Orwell musical haunts the dark disco of '1984', the shape-shifting 'We Are the Dead' and 'Big Brother', which starts off as a melancholy slice of soul but rapidly becomes something more terrifying, with Bowie peeling off awful visions line by line.

The spectre of Orwell's *Nineteen Eighty-Four* is never far away. The closing 'Chant of the Ever-Circling Skeletal Family' presents the prospect of the blasted Earth after Armageddon, with shifting time signatures (5/4 to 6/4) that form a claustrophobic loop. At the end, it locks into a juddering repetition of the first half of the word 'brother' – a neat aural analogy for a chilling line from the novel: 'If you want a picture of the future, imagine a boot stamping on a human face – for ever.'

LEFT – David Robert Jones in 1955, by which time his family were living at 4 Plaistow Grove in Bromley and he was a pupil at Burnt Ash School.

BELOW – David the teenage saxophonist (bottom right) with his band the Kon-Rads in February 1963. At the time he went by the stage name David Jay.

Sporting a hairnet (front right), and flanked by the Manish Boys, David Jones poses for the cameras prior to an appearance on the BBC's *Gadzooks!* show on 8 March 1965, where they played 'I Pity the Fool'. Manager Les Conn had concocted a publicity stunt to promote David's TV musical debut: a story that the BBC wouldn't let the band play unless they had their hair cut.

The eyes have it. Bowie during the mid-sixties. In 1962, during an altercation over a girl, David's friend George Underwood punched him, inadvertently damaging the muscles in his left eye. His pupil became permanently dilated, though his eyesight was unaffected, giving the impression that his eyes were different colours, a slightly unsettling effect that would only enhance the startling look of Ziggy Stardust a few years down the line.

ABOVE – Bowie in 1969 alongside his then girlfriend Hermione Farthingale, and guitarist John 'Hutch' Hutchinson, as the 'multimedia' trio Feathers. He'd had his hair cut for a blink-and-you'll-miss it part in the film *The Virgin Soldiers* the year before.

OPPOSITE, TOP – Bowie at Haddon Hall, Beckenham, in April 1971. He's wearing his infamous 'man dress', bought from the Mr Fish boutique.

OPPOSITE BELOW – Ziggy Stardust and the Spiders from Mars. From left to right: Mick Ronson, Trevor Bolder, David Bowie and Woody Woodmansey. The image comes from photographer Mick Rock's memorable video for 'The Jean Jeanie', made in San Francisco on 28 October 1972.

Getting up close and personal with Mick Ronson's guitar at Hammersmith Odeon, London, in July 1973. Alert to the publicity value of an outrageous gimmick (he was, after all, the son of a PR man), Bowie had first performed the act in 1972, the year he told *Melody Maker* that he was gay. He also encouraged Ronson to pretend that he was gay, but the guitarist gave him short shrift.

Photographer Terry O'Neill captured this iconic image of
Bowie and canine friend during a shoot in 1974. The dog was perfectly calm
most of the time, but O'Neill's strobe light set it off barking, leaping into
the air and straining at its leash. 'David didn't even blink,' recalled O'Neill.
The book at his feet is a late fifties edition of Walter Ross's *The Immortal*,
the story of a wild teen movie idol dead before his time. Modelled on
James Dean, it doubtless resonated with Bowie in the wake of Ziggymania.

The Bowies: David, son Zowie and wife Angie at the Amstel Hotel in
Amsterdam in February 1974. He'd gone to Holland to collect an Edison Award
for the previous year's *The Rise and Fall of Ziggy Stardust and the Spiders from
Mars*. Why the eyepatch? According to Bowie himself, he'd had conjunctivitis
and, with an interview scheduled, wore the patch to cover it up.
But he liked the effect and continued to wear it for a while.

At the Grammy Awards in March 1975 with Yoko Ono and John Lennon.
Bowie scored his first US No. 1 that year with 'Fame', written with the ex-Beatle
(whom he'd only met that year) and guitarist Carlos Alomar. It was through chatting
to Lennon that Bowie began to think of dispensing with a manager altogether.

ABOVE – Bowie as Thomas Jerome Newton on the set
of *The Man Who Fell to Earth* in the summer of 1975.

OPPOSITE – The Thin White Duke onstage in 1976. A cold, aristocratic presence,
the character appears on the album *Station to Station*. The Duke's look – smart
white shirts, black waistcoat and trousers, slicked-back hair – hinted at a bygone
era of elegance (and decadence). Coupled with the Brechtian monochrome stage
set and stark lighting for the accompanying tour, it hinted at Bowie's return to
Europe, a relocation made partly to help him kick his cocaine addiction.

With King Crimson guitarist Robert Fripp and Brian Eno at Hansa Studio in West Berlin, 1977. Fripp recorded all his parts for the *"Heroes"* album during a 48-hour stopover in the city, including the memorable feedback solos on the title track.

Although he'd never acted before, electronica pioneer Ryuichi Sakamoto starred alongside Bowie in 1982's prisoner-of-war movie *Merry Christmas, Mr Lawrence*. In later years, both were living in downtown New York at the same time, although they never met up – 'My great regret,' Sakamoto admitted to the *Guardian* in 2018.

Bowie enjoyed huge mainstream success with 1983's *Let's Dance*, which was supported by the lucrative seven-month 'Serious Moonlight' tour. As part of the set, Bowie revived the staging of 'Cracked Actor' that he'd debuted during his 1974 US tour (and which was filmed for Alan Yentob's 1975 documentary of the same name), in which he dons a cape and sunglasses and sings to a skull.

TOP – On stage during the star-studded Live Aid concert at London's Wembley stadium on 13 July 1985. Bowie's four-song set came after Queen's legendary performance, but he held his own, capturing the spirit of the day perfectly with its finale: "Heroes".

ABOVE – Bowie with wife Iman in the 1990s. In her, he finally found emotional contentment after years of affairs, short-term relationships and long periods of loneliness.

TOP – On stage during the 'A Reality' tour, which kicked off in October 2003. Critics praised Bowie's strong performances, but the long run took its toll on him and he had bouts of sickness. After a gig at the Hurricane Festival in Scheessel, Germany, in June 2004, he collapsed; it was discovered that he had a blocked artery. The remaining dates were cancelled.

ABOVE – With characteristic panache, Bowie released another game-changing album, *Blackstar*, just days before his death in January 2016. The videos for the singles 'Blackstar' (above) and 'Lazarus' – both directed by Johan Renck – were brimful of cryptic, occasionally disturbing imagery that sticks in the mind. What did it all mean? A consummate artist, Bowie kept us guessing right to the end.

There are harbingers of future glories, too, not least in the remarkable medley 'Sweet Thing'/'Candidate'/'Sweet Thing (Reprise)'. Nearly nine minutes long but always absorbing, it anticipates *Station to Station*'s title track. Bowie ponders the dangers of addictive promiscuity (something of a specialist subject for him), running through a showcase of vocal stylings from a deep Scott Walker-esque baritone to impassioned yowps. Mike Garson's piano provides an elegant counterpoint to the guitar distortion.

The sleeve of *Diamond Dogs* shows Ziggy's final incarnation: Halloween Jack as a human-canine hybrid. Based on a photograph by Terry O'Neill, it was created by Guy Peellaert, a Belgian artist who'd been picked to provide the cover for the next Rolling Stones album (*It's Only Rock 'n' Roll*); Bowie engaged in smart one-upmanship to get there three months earlier. The album did good business (UK No. 1, US No. 5) and heralded his most ambitious tour yet, presaged by a Defries press blitz that included billboards on Sunset Strip and Times Square. The $400,000 stage set, featuring the 9-metre skyscrapers and bridges of Hunger City, took a 30-man crew an entire day to raise. With the weight of the performance now resting solely on his shoulders, Bowie amped up the theatricality. Stage front, he was lassoed by dancers during 'Diamond Dogs' and carried out above the audience on a cherry-picker for 'Space Oddity'; elsewhere, he French-kissed a skull for 'Cracked Actor', a caped Hamlet for the demi-monde.

The unenviable task of replacing Mick Ronson fell to 21-year-old Earl Slick, although, like the Spiders before him, the youngster was deeply unhappy at the pay ($300 per week). Bowie also made the acquaintance of another guitarist who was to work with him for the next 15 years on some of his greatest records. Carlos Alomar had played on a Lulu session Bowie had produced at RCA in New York (it yielded her unreleased take on his 'Can You Hear Me?'), and they swiftly bonded. Bowie made it clear that he wanted to know more about contemporary R&B, soul and Latino music, and Alomar, who'd been the youngest guitarist in the house band at Harlem's famous Apollo Theatre, willingly obliged. Taken aback by the singer's skinny frame, he also took Bowie home so that his wife could give him a square meal.

Bowie's burgeoning interest in contemporary black music made him a devotee of Don Cornelius's celebrated TV show *Soul Train* and a student of the Sound of Philadelphia, spearheaded by the songwriting team of Kenneth Gamble and Leon A. Huff. It also influenced a change in vocal style, adding greater depth and vibrato, and a new look: hair flopped into a parting; double-breasted suits with baggy trousers. Bowie's latest girlfriend, Ava Cherry, was a stunning black singer and model who helped him to navigate this untried world. Her father had played in bands during the forties, and she gave Bowie some of his old suits, including voluminous trousers with braces, a style that had been assimilated by African-American teenagers in Chicago in the sixties as the so-called 'gouster' look. Bowie and Angie were married in name only, but she'd often react angrily, and dramatically, to evidence of his affairs. Arriving in Philadelphia, and learning about Cherry, she made as if to throw herself from a hotel window.

Cocaine's capacity for energizing its user was always going to appeal to the stimulation-hungry Bowie, who perhaps saw it in the same vein as the amphetamines his mod peers had popped. ('I'd done a lot of pills ever since I was a kid,' he told *Playboy* in 1976. 'Thirteen or 14.') He was using regularly by late 1973, and his habit escalated once he'd moved to America. His burgeoning use of the drug had an impact not only on the lyrics of *Diamond Dogs*, but also its layered overdubs and thick sound, a world away from the cleaner, more precise ambience of *Hunky Dory* or *Ziggy Stardust*. In July 1974, during a coked-up conversation with MainMan's US president, Tony Zanetta, he finally grasped what the terms of his contract meant. He didn't own half the company; he was entitled only to half of the revenue he'd generated *after* expenses were deducted. And he had no share in the profits from any of MainMan's other operations. He was footing the huge costs of the tour, and many of the company's day-to-day bills, himself. *That's* why this rock superstar was broke.

David Live, his first in-concert album, caught Bowie at a Philadelphia gig in July, transitioning from glam rock to pseudo soul star while in the throes of his cocaine addiction. Mostly it sounds overwrought, although the LP gave him a Top 10 hit on both sides of the Atlantic. On 2 November 1974 he made a twitchy appearance on *The Dick Cavett Show*, prodding the ground before him with a cane (another gouster accoutrement), which he never relinquished, as if it were a talisman. He was worryingly thin, his vibrant orange hair the healthiest thing about him.

The one shining positive at this time was the presence of Corinne 'Coco' Schwab, who joined the typing pool in MainMan's London office but would become Bowie's PA, a role that she would maintain – showing fierce loyalty and protectiveness towards the singer – for decades. She moved to the States with Bowie in early 1974, becoming, along with George Underwood and Geoff MacCormack, one of his very few close, long-term friends. Her devotion, paired with formidable organizational skills, meant that her influence on Bowie's life grew steadily, something that was deeply resented by Angie and Tony Defries, among others.

The tour broke for six weeks, and the restless Bowie decamped to Philadelphia. He invited Alomar to pull together a band, including the former drummer for Sly and the Family Stone, Andy Newmark, for new recordings at the city's Sigma Sound Studios. Alomar brought along his wife, Robin Clark, who was a singer, and her friend Luther Vandross; Cherry also sang. The strong, soul-and-funk-inflected set included 'Young Americans', the ballads 'It's Gonna Be Me' and 'Who Can I Be Now?', a new version of the bisexually inclined 'John, I'm Only Dancing' with revised lyrics, and 'Can You Hear Me?'. Having rekindled his relationship with Bowie by mixing *Diamond Dogs* (which Bowie had produced himself) and *David Live*, Tony Visconti was invited back as producer.

When the tour resumed, it had been transformed in the light of the Sigma Sound sessions. Alomar joined the band to up the funk quota, while Vandross and Cherry provided backing vocals. The Flares' track 'Footstompin'' (1961) joined the set, alongside a cover of Eddie Floyd's

'Knock on Wood'. As the troupe moved east, through the Midwest, the elaborate and costly Hunger City set was axed; by late October the tour had become a soul revue. Dubbed *Philly Dogs*, it debuted some of the songs Bowie had been working on at Sigma, doubtless puzzling fans who'd turned up expecting to hear material from *Diamond Dogs*. The forthcoming LP's working title was 'Shilling the Rubes' – a reference to conning a crowd into buying a sham product, in a tongue-in-cheek reference to what Bowie dubbed his 'plastic soul' – and later 'The Gouster'. In December Bowie decamped to New York's Hit Factory to finish the last two tracks, 'Fascination' and 'Win'.

In early January 1975 a delighted Visconti took the master tapes back to London for mixing and to add strings. But the album had an unplanned late lease of life after Bowie coaxed ex-Beatle John Lennon down to Electric Lady studios the very day Visconti flew out. Jamming on 'Footstompin'', to which Alomar had added a riff from the Rascals' 'Jungle Walk', they came up with a taut, funky meditation on the perils of stardom: 'Fame'. It was one of two surprise last-minute additions to the album, the second a clunky cover of the Beatles' 'Across the Universe'. Visconti was shocked when he heard the revised album, *sans* his favourites 'Who Can I Be Now?' and 'It's Gonna Be Me', both sacrificed for the new tracks. 'Beautiful songs,' he mourned, 'and it made me sick when he decided not to use them.'

This year's Bowie, as seen on the *Young Americans* sleeve, was a blow-dried, airbrushed movie idol, with smoke snaking from his cigarette. Released on 7 March 1975, the album is a divisive entry in his catalogue. The singer himself frequently dissed it, once referring to it as 'the phoniest R&B I've ever heard', while his early champion Michael Watts in *Melody Maker* complained that 'He patently lacks any deep emotional connection to his material.' But that's to dismiss the stellar playing from an exceptional band, and Bowie's own song-writing. 'Fascination' and the gospel-tinged title track – his impressions of post-Watergate America, incorporating a nod to the Beatles' 'A Day in the Life' – offer exuberant examples of blue-eyed soul. The vocal backing throughout is inspired, from the syncopated repeats of the song title in 'Young Americans' to the complex to-and-fro interplay on 'Right', one of several sultry ballads including 'Can You Hear Me?' and 'Win'. And James Brown offered 'Fame' the ultimate backhanded compliment by copying it on his single 'Hot' in January 1976.

During this period Bowie and Lennon also compared notes on management and publishing, as a result of which Bowie realized belatedly that he controlled his master tapes only as long as he remained with MainMan. At the end of January he employed Michael Lippman, an entertainment lawyer who was to become his next manager, to sever him from Defries, although one of his earlier mentors, the endearingly grudge-free Kenneth Pitt, generously contributed advice. The tortuous ensuing lawsuit ran on during 1975. Its settlement resulted in Bowie surrendering a 16 per cent royalty to MainMan on any new material composed up to 30 September 1982, and 50 per cent of any future earnings on past recordings up to *David Live*, including his Decca material. Dauntingly, MainMan retained control of his masters. That said, Defries had done what he'd said he'd do: make Bowie a star. 'Fame' gave the singer his first US No. 1, even as he was parting company with his manager.

* * * * *

During the summer of 1974 Alan Yentob made a remarkable and revealing film about Bowie. Broadcast on BBC TV in January 1975, *Cracked Actor* showed his on-stage brilliance, while off-stage he proved a candid and compelling interviewee. But his cocaine addiction was by now obvious, not least in his habitual sniffs. In one scene, en route to a gig, a police car prompts nervous chatter. In another, as Bowie is being chauffeured across the Californian desert – his aviophobia still unshakeable – Yentob asks him about his assimilation of American culture. Bowie replies that a fly has just landed in the carton of milk he's drinking from. 'It's a foreign body … and it's getting a lot of milk! It's kind of how I feel – a foreign body here and I couldn't help but soak it up.'

The documentary effectively served as an audition reel for Bowie's most highly regarded movie role. The casting agent Maggie Abbott had brought Mick Jagger to the director Nicolas Roeg's attention for *Performance* (1970), a bleak coda to the sixties and Jagger's strongest cinematic outing. Now she gave Roeg a tape of *Cracked Actor*, which swiftly convinced him and producer Si Litvinoff of Bowie's suitability to play the lead in a movie they were casting, *The Man Who Fell to Earth*. The part was that of Thomas Jerome Newton, an alien who arrives from a planet suffering devastating drought. (Jagger was briefly considered for the role.) To generate funds for transporting water back home, Newton employs his knowledge of advanced technology to create valuable patents that make him wealthy.

But he becomes side-tracked, discovering alcohol, sex and TV, and is then subjected to invasive medical tests by suspicious government forces. At the end, he is still young, still wealthy, but now a depressive alcoholic.

In preparation for the shoot, which would take place in New Mexico, to be nearer Lippman, and doubtless further away from Angie (and Cherry, herself increasingly angry at his philandering), Bowie moved to Los Angeles in the spring. Aside from filming, he would remain there for the next ten months. His funds were low after the recent litigation, and his settlement with MainMan would curtail royalties from his recordings, so to economize he stayed with friends and acquaintances. He moved in with the Deep Purple guitarist Glenn Hughes, who had a house in Beverly Hills, during the spring of 1975, immersing himself in books about the occult, numerology and the Jewish Kabbalah. Both men were hooked on cocaine, but they weren't going to clubs, despite coke's reputation as a party drug. They hardly left the house. Sustained by the white lines, Bowie would stay up for days on end watching Fritz Lang movies or documentaries on the Nazis, obsessed by their appropriation of the ancient swastika symbol – which, as he probably already knew, to Buddhists signifies good fortune as well as the Buddha's footprints and heart. He also became intrigued by the theory – which he'd come across in Trevor Ravenscroft's book *The Spear of Destiny* (1973) – that they had been trying to locate the Holy Grail. Unhelpfully, Hughes's home was not far from the site of the shocking murders carried out by Charles Manson's 'Family' in 1969; when he found out, an increasingly paranoid Bowie hid all the knives.

In June, during an interview with Cameron Crowe for *Playboy*, he became convinced that he'd seen a body falling outside the window.

Bowie found the sprawling new city somewhat over-whelming and difficult to navigate, but fascinating all the same. He took Crowe on a whirlwind morning ride in a Volkswagen Beetle. 'His eyes never stop scanning the streets,' noted Crowe. 'He thrills over the massage parlours, billboards and stumbling itinerants.' For someone with an insatiable, pan-cultural curiosity, the city was ripe for study. 'LA is my favourite museum,' Bowie told Crowe. He enthusiastically regaled the reporter with a non-stop litany of mooted projects (screenplays he'd written, plans to direct Terence Stamp with Iggy Pop), possibly not unconnected with the fact that his cocaine habit was now ballooning: 'I like fast drugs,' he confessed to Crowe. 'I hate anything that slows me down.' That was thanks largely to the purity of the powder supplied by the dealer Freddie Sessler, a lively raconteur who was part of the Rolling Stones' inner circle and a close friend and confidant of Keith Richards. It was commonplace in Los Angeles at the time to see silver coke spoons dangling from necklaces worn by people in the music industry. The damaging effects of the drug weren't yet fully appreciated, or at least not taken seriously.

By June, Bowie was living in Lippman's Hollywood home. Later he rented a bizarre cubic white house at 637 North Doheny Drive, built around an indoor swimming pool and decorated with Egyptian touches, including a pair of mini sphinxes guarding the front steps. His diet at the time consisted largely of cocaine, milk and peppers; unsurprisingly, his weight plummeted below 45 kg, something that alarmed Schwab, who strove to keep him nourished and as healthy as she could, fulfilling the hybrid role of friend, mother and sometime lover. 'I've got to put more weight on that boy,' she fretted to Crowe at a Los Angeles supermarket, as she popped cartons of extra-rich milk into her basket. At the height of his psychosis, she'd wake in the morning, pad over to his sleeping form and place the mirror he'd been snorting coke off in front of his nose to see if he was still breathing.

The Man Who Fell to Earth premiered at London's Leicester Square Theatre on 18 March 1976. It proved a fascinating if flawed work, although the cuts later instigated for US distribution, without Roeg's knowledge, hardly added clarity. Reviewers expressed themselves either bewildered or turned off. But Bowie was an inspired choice, exuding a curiously distant presence: 'Some days my face would ache through not being able to use it and having to be absolutely expressionless,' he recalled. And he looked extraordinary, arrestingly pale, his hair sculpted into a flaming coiffure by the British hairdresser Martin Samuel. The designer Ola Hudson, mother of Guns N' Roses guitarist Slash and another of Bowie's lovers, injected a whiff of vintage Hollywood glamour into his wardrobe, pairing smart single-breasted suits with dress shirts and fedoras.

* * * * *

Bowie appears in a monochrome still from *The Man Who Fell to Earth* on the cover of his tenth studio LP, released on 23 January 1976. *Station to Station* proved a phenomenal achievement, especially considering his fragile mental state. 'I was amazed how he could come up with that, having been in complete cocaine psychosis,' Hughes marvelled. Well, those were the times – and they affect the principal cast's memories of the album's recording sessions. Bowie himself said he remembered next to nothing. The infectious hook to 'Golden Years' – joyous disco doo-wop, and a transatlantic Top 10 hit in November 1975 – was possibly influenced by the opening riff to Wilson Pickett's hit 'Funky Broadway' (1967). But was it Carlos Alomar or Earl Slick who came up with it? Perhaps the songs were planned before recording at Hollywood's Cherokee Studios; perhaps they evolved in the studio, like most of Bowie's albums of the time. But all agree that Bowie's work ethic was iron-clad; the music was all, and if that meant hauling a guitarist out of bed, or a bar, in the middle of the night, so be it.

The sound of a steam train kicks off three minutes of sonic adventurism on the title track before the vocals enter. The journey is spiritual rather than physical; Bowie pointed out that the title references the Stations of the Cross, scenes from Christ's journey to crucifixion on Calvary. But the lyrics also name-check Kether (relating to the divine realm) and Malkuth (relating to the physical world), endpoints on the Kabbalistic Tree of Life. As much as anything, the song charts a course for Bowie from the madness of his Los Angeles sojourn towards something calmer and life-affirming. Given his fragile state of mind at the time, it's no surprise to find 'Word on a Wing' here, an impassioned offering that the troubled star described as both a 'hymn' and 'safeguard'. The bizarre 'TVC15', inspired partly by a hallucinating Iggy's impression that his television was eating his girlfriend, pairs a sentimental croon with honky-tonk piano and a thundering chorus.

Bowie was a great admirer of Nina Simone, a songwriter and interpreter of astounding depth and a prodigiously gifted pianist. In 1974 she was facing existential struggles of her own, and many felt that the pressure the US Inland Revenue Service was bringing to bear on her was not unrelated to her outspoken civil rights campaigning. She'd taken her daughter to see a Bowie show at Madison Square Garden that July, and afterwards bumped into him at a private club. Bowie took her number, then phoned her at 3 am. Over the following month they engaged in long telephone conversations, during which Bowie told her that she was a genius, working on an altogether different level from himself, and giving her invaluable support and reassurance at a time when she badly needed it. *Station to Station* ends with 'Wild Is the Wind', a stunning example of Bowie's interpretive ability and vocal control, his inspiration Simone's own spare, melancholy version from 1966.

The supporting *Isolar* tour ran from February to May 1976, from North America to Europe, and was roundly celebrated, not least for its stark, Brechtian staging of fluorescent white lights against black backdrops. To set the avant-garde Euro-tone, evenings began with music from Kraftwerk's album *Radioactivity*, followed by a showing of the classic Surrealist movie *Un Chien Andalou*, directed by Salvador Dalí and Luis Buñuel. The monochrome staging was complemented by Bowie's stage costume: a crisp white shirt with fitted black waistcoat and high-waisted, loose trousers (Ola Hudson's work again). Glam had become old-school glamour, complemented by a slicked-back hairdo. Introduced in the opening line of 'Station to Station', Bowie's latest alter ego, Thin White Duke, was a hollow and amoral aristocrat, born in part from Bowie's snow-blind existence in Los Angeles but also anticipating the next stage of his career, in which he swapped American R&B and soul for the new Europeanism epitomized by Kraftwerk, Neu! and Faust. In 1977 he would tell *Melody Maker* that *Station to Station* 'was like a plea to come back to Europe for me'.

The tour began on 2 February in Vancouver and wound through the continent to a triumphant close at Madison Square Garden, New York, on 26 March. Along the way it picked up Iggy Pop, who would become Bowie's travelling companion and, over the following years, confidant. Even in the midst of his cocaine blizzard, Bowie had retained something of his compassionate best, as his calls to Simone attested. He had been one of very few people to visit Iggy when he'd been a patient at UCLA's Neuropsychiatric Institute after MainMan dumped him, and where he'd been diagnosed with a combination of narcissism and bipolar disorder. Both men were acutely aware of the need to get clean and refocus their lives, although that would be years in the making – and not without setbacks for each of them.

Station to Station went Top 5 in both the UK and the USA, concerts were packed and Bowie's band was exceptional – witness the recording made at Nassau Coliseum on 23 March (and officially released in 2010). After his show on 11 February at the Forum in Inglewood, Los Angeles, he chatted to the writer Christopher Isherwood backstage.

Isherwood had evocatively brought to life his experience of living in the German city during the Weimar Republic of the twenties – a strange brew of dissolute nightlife and the encroaching shadow of fascism – in his novels *Mr Norris Changes Trains* (1935) and *Goodbye to Berlin* (1939); the latter was the source for the film musical *Cabaret* in 1972. By the end of the tour, the singer had resolved to move to the city, taking Iggy with him.

Bowie hadn't played live in the UK since his Ziggy days. But, despite the feverish anticipation, things got off to a potentially catastrophic start. Arriving at Victoria railway station on 2 May, he waved to fans while standing in the back of his open-topped black Mercedes-Benz. But when photographs of the day were published, some commentators likened his gesture to a Nazi salute. It didn't help that members of Hitler's elite also favoured convertible Mercedes-Benzes. The *Führer*'s choice was the 770K Grosser Offener Tourenwagen (W150), while Bowie had recently bought a 600 Pullman State Landaulet limousine.

It was an unlucky accident, but given unwanted credence by Bowie's unfortunate flirtations with fascism at the time. In 1974 he'd told *Playboy* that 'Adolf Hitler was one of the first rock stars … I think he was quite as good as Jagger … He was a media artist himself.' And, at a press conference in Stockholm in April 1976: 'I believe Britain could benefit from a fascist leader. After all, fascism is really nationalism.' There's little doubt that Bowie was neither racist nor anti-Semitic – a quick survey of his lovers and the musicians he worked with should put paid to that notion. But he *was* a voracious reader with a vast intellectual appetite, a racing mind and (at the time) a prodigious drug addiction, all of which conspired to let his tongue run away with itself before his brain could intervene. He acknowledged as much himself in 1983, telling *NME*: 'After I've written something, or when I've started writing something, I then try to intellectualise what I'm doing. And that's when the problems usually begin. Especially … when you've just done a gram of cocaine.'

None of this affected the success of the *Isolar* tour, which culminated in two triumphant shows at the Pavillon de Paris in May. Thereafter Bowie took up an offer to escape the attention of fans and journalists with a break at the Château d'Hérouville, which he'd last visited for the *Pin Ups* sessions. While there, he would also begin work on Iggy's new album, *The Idiot*, which would allow him to road-test ideas for his next benchmark in forward-thinking pop.

7

Berlin Calling

The finishing touches were added to *The Idiot* in Berlin's Hansa Studio 1 and included a final mix by Tony Visconti. The producer's return to the fold had been prompted by a phone call from Bowie during the summer of 1976 to ask if he was available for a project he was planning, with Brian Eno in tow, that might or might not result in anything. Visconti was delighted, and to whet their appetites he informed them that he would be bringing along a machine that 'fucks with the fabric of time'.[1]

Following two weeks of jamming featuring the core of Bowie's go-to crew at the time (Carlos Alomar, percussionist Dennis Davis and bass player George Murray), the musicians left and the party slimmed down to Visconti, Bowie and Eno. The last-named had brought his own box of tricks: his then rare EMS Synthi AKS synthesizer, housed in its own briefcase. During the final two weeks of September they focused on what would become the instrumental-only side of Bowie's next album.

Less happily, Bowie occasionally had to head back to Paris to deal with lawyers. In January he'd instigated a $2 million lawsuit against his now ex-manager Michael

---

[1] More prosaically, the Eventide 910 Harmonizer allows its user to alter the pitch of a sound in real time.

Lippman over taking a higher commission than expected and withholding funds; Lippman countersued, also for £2 million. With his royalties frozen during the legal discussions, Bowie was in dire financial straits, telling *Melody Maker*'s Chris Charlesworth flatly: 'Making a bit of money is my prime interest' and 'I never made any money from that [*Diamond Dogs*] tour … I'm managing myself now, simply because I've got fed up with managers that I've known.'[2] Coco Schwab did much to fill that vacuum, mixing formidable organizational skill and a deep affection for Bowie with a no-nonsense protectiveness that didn't sit well with everyone – including band members, whom she hired and fired, and took to task if she felt they were a bad influence on him, especially with regard to drugs. At around the same time Bowie resolved to take a more responsible attitude towards his son's upbringing, and to spend more time with him, to the point of taking time off touring. He'd brought Zowie to the chateau for the recording sessions, with his Scottish nanny, Marion Skene, who would become something of a surrogate mother to the boy over the following years. Bowie relished having him there. 'At first, [having a son] frightened me, and I tried not to see the implications,' he admitted to *Melody Maker*. 'Now it's *his* future that concerns me.'

It was Schwab who found the seven-room apartment at 155 Hauptstrasse in Berlin's Schöneberg, an unfashionable

---

[2] Partly inspired by conversations with John Lennon, in the late seventies Bowie would dispense with having a manager altogether, relying instead on a pared-down circle of advisers that included Coco Schwab.

district with a lively gay community, that would become his new home; Iggy Pop became his flatmate. Bowie took genuine pleasure in Berlin (and its affordability). Sometimes accompanied by Iggy and Schwab, he'd shop for books, or art in Nollendorfplatz and Winterfeldtplatz, or explore the streets Christopher Isherwood had known. He might drop in to the nearby gay-friendly Anderes Ufer for a coffee, soak up the intellectual to-and-fro at the Café Exil, or eat out at Paris Bar. Naturally, he and Iggy sought out the cabarets and gay clubs, but he also cycled, while Iggy rose early and walked the city for miles. Old coke habits die hard, and they'd still indulge, sometimes at the SO36 club; but they boozed rather more, at the Unlimited on the Kurfürstendamm and the Dschungel cocktail bar, where a sozzled Iggy would treat the customers to Frank Sinatra medleys. Bowie's years of drug abuse had left him physically fragile, though, and during one ferocious argument with Angie, probably over Schwab and her increasing influence on him, he collapsed with chest pains.

More positively, Bowie started painting, producing a large Expressionist portrait of the Japanese writer Yukio Mishima that he hung above his bed. He and Iggy visited the city's Die Brücke Museum, a repository of Expressionist works condemned as 'degenerate' by the Third Reich, although Bowie continued to seek out Nazi memorabilia in the city's junk shops, too, apparently without sensing any contradiction. He and Iggy wore casual streetwear – jeans, checked shirts and flat caps, workman's overalls from a shop on the Mehringdamm – dressing down to blend in. Whether Bowie the English rock star could ever be truly anonymous there is a moot point, but he was left alone and began to piece together his life, later paying tribute to 'a joy of life … a great feeling of release and healing' that the city allowed him.

Soon enough Berlin helped to dispel Bowie's fascination with the Nazis; after all, he was now mixing with people whose fathers had served in the SS ('That was a good way to be woken up out of that particular dilemma'). Curiously, he showed little interest in the vibrant contemporary counterculture of the city, whose residents were not required to do military service, a fact that attracted more than the usual number of bohemian youths. Instead, he gravitated towards the past, the between-the-wars era of the Weimar Republic. He'd take visitors around the 'TischTelefon' bars, where guests could still make rendezvous with each other via table-top Bakelite telephones. Less positively, his marriage with Angie was coming to an ugly end, exacerbated by her habit of bringing her latest boyfriend into the studio – although in general she disliked Berlin and preferred to remain in their new family home. (The Bowies had bought a chalet in Blonay not far from Montreux, in 1976, not least because of Switzerland's lenient tax rates.) In between recordings, Bowie had to contend with divorce proceedings and custody hearings over his son, alongside his continuing legal squabbles with Lippman.

Completed at the recently opened Hansa Studio by the Wall in West Berlin, *Low* was released on 14 January 1977. The LP's two sides represented different worlds, not unlike the city Bowie had made his new home. Side A is mostly song-based, although they're a heterogeneous lot. 'Speed of Life' is the briefest of overtures, a motorik rocker in the vein of Neu! or Faust. Intriguingly, Bowie's first choice for the album's guitarist had been Neu!'s Michael Rother ('Neu! being passionate, even diametrically opposed to Kraftwerk', as Bowie later observed). In the event, Ricky Gardiner's left-field contributions became a highlight of *Low*'s first side.

The fallout from Bowie's marital problems was never far away. Carlos Alomar recalls Bowie bickering ferociously with Angie and creating the arrangement for 'Breaking Glass' to mirror an argument; and Bowie's lyrics mix references to their strife with an oblique nod to the occult ramblings of his Los Angeles period. 'Be My Wife' expresses a longing for a stable home and partner. The English boogie-woogie maestro Roy Young contributes rollicking piano, and Bowie once more airs his Anthony Newleyisms; the overall effect is not unlike a Blur song *c*.1994.

'Sound and Vision' is *Low*'s most commercial- and coherent-sounding track, and gave him a UK No. 3. Eminently dance-friendly, if oddly lopsided (like much of Side A), it's just one verse and two choruses long, with lyrics that suggest an almost catatonic withdrawal, blinds drawn against the daylight, a lyrical memento of Bowie's cocooned world of drug abuse in Los Angeles. Visconti created the brutal, gated drum sound using his Eventide Harmonizer, providing one of *Low*'s sonic signatures and birthing a hallmark of eighties pop production.

'Always Crashing in the Same Car' might have been inspired by an event in which Bowie repeatedly rammed his fifties Mercedes into that of a drug dealer who'd conned him. Or by his speeding recklessly around a West Berlin garage in a suicide attempt. Either way, his despair at being locked into a rut of destructive behaviour is palpable. The instrumental 'A New Career in a New Town' ends the side on an upbeat note, with Bowie's bluesy harmonica adding a breezy lilt.

Low's largely instrumental second side is a beautiful if bleak quartet, opening with the glacial 'Warszawa', inspired by a grim trip through Poland that Bowie and his entourage had taken earlier in the year. Eno's stately synthesizers are eventually joined by Bowie, emoting in an imaginary language inspired by a recording of a Balkan boys' choir; the effect is equal parts lament and prayer. Bowie later described the sparse 'Art Decade' as a reference to West Berlin and its enforced isolation from outside culture. Its title – also readable as 'art decayed' – isn't the album's only pun: the cover shot, adapted from a still from *The Man Who Fell to Earth*, works with the title as 'low profile', a nod to Bowie's new understated exist-ence. 'Weeping Wall' features xylophones, guitar, piano and vibraphones, all played by Bowie, in a repetitively mesmeric composition influenced by the minimalist master Philip Glass. The title refers both to Jerusalem's Wailing Wall and to the infamous line dividing Berlin. 'Subterraneans' switches its gaze to East Berlin, with snatches of Bowie's jazzy saxophone offering a snapshot of life before the Wall went up.

Bowie sent Nicolas Roeg a copy of the album, telling him that it was the kind of thing he'd had in mind as a soundtrack for *The Man Who Fell to Earth*. He had originally been commissioned to provide music for the movie, but the sessions stalled after two months. As so often happens when it comes to discussing David Bowie – particularly during this intense and eventful period

– there are several versions of what happened. His cocaine dependency probably played its part, although he produced some stunning work (including *Station to Station*) while an addict. Some reports suggest that Roeg didn't like the synthesizer-based sounds Bowie was coming up with; others disagree. The producer Si Litvinoff thought it was all because Bowie had been asked to take a pay cut. Five years later Bowie himself fumed to *NME*: 'I was under the impression that I'd be writing [all of] the music for the film. I was then told that if I would care to submit my music along with other people's … and I just said "Shit, you're not getting any of it."'

Low was a hit (UK No. 2; US No. 11), although a perplexed and disappointed RCA gave it little promotion. They even held it back until the start of the new year, a dead time for releases.[3] Trying to make sense of the album, *NME* printed two reviews, neither wholeheartedly positive. At least for Ian MacDonald, *Low* was 'the *only* contemporary rock album'. But Charles Shaar Murray deplored its nihilism and passivity: 'This album doesn't exorcise psychotic withdrawal by externalisation and catharsis,' he complained. 'It induces such a state, reinforces it, beckons to the lemmings.' Murray contrasted *Low*'s perceived shortcomings with the vibrant anger of contemporary Sex Pistols records – to him, a violent but necessary wiping clean of the slate. Bowie had coincidentally abandoned the UK and USA during the rise

---

[3] Bowie opted not to take *Low* on the road, preferring instead to play keyboards on Iggy's 'The Idiot' tour. Its sprawling itinerary forced him – on 10 March 1977 – to take a flight for the first time since 1972, and he was soon flying regularly again.

of punk. But with *Low* he was already inspiring what would come next: the sound of John Foxx-era Ultravox, for example, or the dark post-punk of Joy Division, whose original name – Warsaw – nodded to *Low*'s 'Warszawa'. For Joy Division's debut EP, *An Ideal for Living*, their drummer Stephen Morris asked the engineer to re-create the drum sound on 'Speed of Life'. (He couldn't.) The Cure's Robert Smith acknowledged the synth textures of *Low* as an influence on the icy textures of their album *17 Seconds*. And in their pre-hit, post-punk incarnation, the Psychedelic Furs' sound drew heavily on Bowie's Berlin era, while Richard Butler's vocals were steeped in the master's own. As George Walden observes in *Who's a Dandy?*, 'In the mass age, the true original is the man who looks and behaves today in the way that everyone will look and behave tomorrow.'

Much of the recording for *Low* took place in the French countryside, at the Château d'Hérouville. Of the albums that make up what has become known as Bowie's 'Berlin Trilogy' (although he preferred the artier 'triptych'), only the next one would be fully realized in the city itself. Using largely the same group of musicians, they rehearsed at the former UFA studios, where Fritz Lang had filmed *Metropolis* and which had subsequently been appropriated for Joseph Goebbels's Nazi propaganda machine. Recordings took place in Hansa's main building (the Studio by the Wall) on Köthener Strasse, some 500 metres from the guard towers and guns; most of the backing tracks were nailed in two days. Eno was a prime influence, not least with his 'Oblique Strategies', a pack of cards devised with his friend the artist Peter Schmidt, bearing suggestive instructions of which possibly the best known is 'Honour thy error as a hidden intention'.

Exchanging a rural setting in France for a divided German city palpably affected the mindset of the musicians. Alomar thought 'the air was thick with a darker vibe' and that Berlin was 'a rather dark, industrial place to work'. Hansa's huge Studio 2, a former concert hall, had once been used by members of the Gestapo as a ballroom, which no doubt played its part. Ironically, given the overall ambience of the record, Eno recalled laughing more during the sessions than on any other. He and Bowie frequently slipped into the foul-mouthed characters Derek and Clive, created by Peter Cook and Dudley Moore, who in the early sixties had become famous while performing in the satirical revue *Beyond the Fringe* before creating the celebrated TV sketch show *Not Only ... But Also*. (John Lennon was a fan, making a handful of appearances.)

Bowie left it until most of the musicians had gone home before concentrating on lyrics, and even then he wound up writing lines just seconds before recording them, a technique he'd gleaned from Iggy. King Crimson's guitarist Robert Fripp made a flying 48-hour visit, and his soaring guitar lines make a singular contribution to the sound of the set. Rather than hearing songs beforehand, he was asked simply to react to the music as he heard it, while Eno mutated the sound with his synth. The result was an astonishing display of reactive, intuitive playing that Visconti wove into composite solos – heard to greatest effect on the album's title track.

Released on 14 October 1977, *"Heroes"* was a brilliant achievement (and a UK No. 3 album). Housed in a sober black-and-white sleeve photographed by Masayoshi Sukita (Bowie's pose was inspired by Erich Heckel's 1917 woodcut *Roquairol*), its brooding themes played out with vibrant energy and sonic inventiveness. The raucous 'Beauty and the Beast' probably acknowledges the damage done during Bowie's Thin White Duke era, and features a backing that recalls both Talking Heads and Kraftwerk, whose Florian Schneider is alluded to in the title of 'V-2 Schneider'.[4] It was a two-way street: the Düsseldorf quartet had name-dropped Bowie and Iggy on *Trans-Europe Express* seven months earlier. The tracks' fervid energy re-emerges in the chaotic riffs of 'Joe the Lion', inspired by the performance artist Chris Burden, whose most notorious piece saw him nailed to the roof of a VW Beetle. 'Blackout' unleashes a panoply of crazy sonics, from Dennis Davis's unhinged workouts to screeching synths; the aural angularity of this song, and of its predecessor, would become a signature feature of post-punk bands.

'Sense of Doubt', the gentle 'Moss Garden', on which Bowie plays a Japanese *koto*, and elegantly downbeat 'Neuköln' – named after a Berlin district (Neukölln) where

---

[4] Bowie might have heard and appreciated German bands, but Brian Eno actually played with them, working with Harmonia in 1976 on the then unreleased *Tracks and Traces* and recording two exquisite albums with Cluster. By contrast, Bowie's mooted collaboration with Tangerine Dream's Edgar Froese on *Low* never came about. Likewise, for reasons that remain unclear, he failed to recruit Neu!'s guitarist Michael Rother for either *Low* or (according to Rother himself) *"Heroes"*.

Turkish migrant workers lived, hence the Middle Eastern modalities – provide a cohesive suite of sparse instrumentals, an echo of *Low*'s ghostly ambient quartet.

"Heroes" dominates, of course, one of Bowie's impassioned vocals over a rush of synths, Fripp's mesmerizing lead guitar and a grinding Velvets-style rhythm. As a song of bullet-proof hope in the face of oppression, it marked how much Bowie's mindset had changed since the days of *The Man Who Sold the World*. One of his best and best-known tracks, it unaccountably flopped in the charts (UK No. 24) but gloriously received its due in 1987 when he played West Berlin on a stage backed up to the Wall itself; on the other side, East Berliners joined in. 'We would hear them cheering and singing along from the other side,' he recalled in 2003, still moved by the thought. 'When we did "Heroes" it really felt anthemic, almost like a prayer.'

Sensing what he'd achieved, Bowie willingly promoted the album. RCA got behind it, too, not least with the memorable advertising slogan: 'There's old wave. There's new wave. And there's David Bowie'. *NME* had no qualms this time, and its reviewer Angus MacKinnon was astonished at the album's 'phenomenally fast event horizon'. *"Heroes"* become the paper's album of the year.

In September 1977 Bowie had reconvened with Marc Bolan on the latter's TV series, in which he introduced teatime viewers to young bands such as Generation X and the Jam. It ended in tragicomedy: the two were jamming on a tune together when an overly refreshed Bolan fell off the platform, leaving a grinning Bowie alone. A few days later and Bowie was off to New York for one of the oddest pairings in his career: a guest spot on Bing Crosby's *Merrie Olde Christmas* holiday show, duetting with the septuagenarian crooner on the festive medley 'Peace on Earth/Little Drummer Boy'. In November he was in the city again to provide the narration for a new recording of Sergei Prokofiev's *Peter and the Wolf.* But nine days later Bowie's mod sidekick and glam-rock rival Bolan was dead, killed in a car crash in Barnes, southwest London. A devastated Bowie attended the funeral later that month, and afterwards passed by his old homes in Brixton and Beckenham. (In a grim coincidence, Crosby had also died that October.) Despite the occasional bitchy quotation in the rock press, mostly from Bolan, their friendship had endured the competitiveness of the glam-rock era. The positively romantic 'Lady Stardust', a glittery delight from *Ziggy Stardust*, was reportedly about the T.Rex star.

Bowie spent Christmas in Berlin with his son and Marion Skene, but without his wife. (In early 1978 an increasingly isolated Angie would make an unsuccessful suicide attempt and sell her bitter story to the *Sunday Mirror.*) Rather than head back into the studio afterwards, he turned once more to acting. Set in 1920s Berlin, David Hemmings's *Just a Gigolo* might have seemed tailor-made for him, but in the event the movie was a dud; Bowie didn't even get to meet his co-star, Marlene Dietrich, a prime motivation for his taking the role. 'You were disappointed and you weren't even in it. Imagine how we felt,' he quipped to *NME* in 1980. 'It was my 32 Elvis Presley movies rolled into one.' At least it showed the diversity he was striving for, summed up in his term 'generalist'.

By the time the live double album *Stage* appeared, in September 1978, work had begun on what became *Lodger*, the last in the trio of LPs loosely connected with Berlin. Bowie and his 'DAM Trio' (Dennis Davis, Carlos Alomar and George Murray) reconvened in Montreux's Mountain Studios, but the magic of the *"Heroes"* sessions proved elusive. The studio was claustrophobic, dubbed a 'concrete bunker' by guitarist Adrian Belew. Alomar was increasingly impatient with Eno's cerebral game-playing, which included directing the band by pointing at chord names written on a board. '[We] did play a number of "art pranks" on the band,' Bowie admitted. 'They really didn't go down too well.' But Eno and Bowie weren't quite gelling either.

Bowie's previous album had closed with the disco-shuffle of 'The Secret Life of Arabia', in which he plays an actor trapped in a movie, and anticipated this last entry in the 'Berlin Trilogy': *Lodger*'s ambience suggested a kind of travelogue, partly influenced by Bowie's recent experiences of Berlin, Kenya and Japan (he'd arrived there for the final dates of his *Isolar II* tour in December and stayed on into January). Joyous non-Western rhythms went into the mix, along with sampling, in which Eno was a leading influence. In 1980 Eno would produce the even more sample-heavy *My Life in the Bush of Ghosts*, a celebrated collaboration with David Byrne, along with *Remain in Light* by Byrne's band Talking Heads. Both married broadly Western 'rock' tropes with those of other cultures.

'Boys Keep Swinging' (a UK No. 7) was a camp garage-rock delight, its clattering sound resulting from Bowie asking each musician to swap his instrument for another that he couldn't properly play. In its memorable video, Bowie drags up as three different women; at the end, he yanks off the wigs, smearing his lipstick across his mouth, a gesture he'd seen at the Lutzower Lampe cabaret club run by the glamorous transsexual Romy Haag, with whom he'd had an affair. Like Fripp on *"Heroes"*, Belew was asked simply to plug in and play on arrival, without first hearing anything; composites of the results light up 'Boys Keep Swinging', 'DJ' and 'Red Sails'.

Bowie's stylized vocal on 'DJ' recalled Byrne's knowingly uptight delivery, He delivers 'Repetition', a tale of domestic abuse, in an appropriately blank tone. 'Look Back in Anger' is a thunderous charge, with Bowie's lead vocal reminiscent of Scott Walker in places, while 'Yassassin' pairs Arabic tonalities with a reggae beat in another tale inspired by the lives of Berlin's Turkish citizens. Incorporating Swahili chants and prepared piano by Eno, 'African Night Flight' took inspiration from the music Bowie heard while on holiday in Kenya with his son. On another album rich in vocal diversity, he unveils the song's scattershot imagery in breathless bursts. When Eno arrived at Montreux, he brought with him the Walker Brothers' 1978 album *Nite Flights*. The four extraordinary tracks written by Scott Walker, whom Bowie greatly admired, were audibly influenced by *Low* and *"Heroes"*, as the title of 'African Night Flight' acknowledges. (Of Walker's quartet, 'The Electrician', a chilling snapshot from a torture cell, made the most enduring impression on Bowie, who would revisit it for 'The Motel' in 1995.)

But spirits waned as the sessions wore on. Perhaps Bowie was tired after the intense creative burst that had produced his previous two landmark albums. Whether because of a paucity of ideas, or an Eno-style compositional shake-up, several tracks were based on existing songs: 'Move On' reverses the chord sequence of 'All the Young Dudes', while the surging 'Fantastic Voyage' borrows the chords and key of 'Boys Keep Swinging', and 'Red Money' adds new lyrics to 'Sister Midnight' from Iggy's album *The Idiot*. To make matters worse, Tony Visconti was given a poorly equipped studio at New York's Record Plant for recording Bowie's vocals and mixing (*Lodger*'s thin mix was roundly criticized; Visconti eventually remixed it for the box set *A New Career in a New Town [1977–1982]*, released in 2017). But anyway, by then – March 1979 – Bowie seemed to be losing interest in the project.

The gatefold cover, at least, showed that his appetite for confrontational art remained healthy. A collaboration with the pop artist Derek Boshier and the photographer Brian Duffy, it took the form of a mock postcard that, when unfolded, revealed Bowie awkwardly splayed as if he'd fallen from a great height, his face a twisted grimace (Duffy's assistants distorted his facial features using fishing wire). It harked back to Bowie's study of mime, but also to the angularity of figures in Expressionist artworks; Egon Schiele's *Self-Portrait as St Sebastian* (1914) was a likely influence. RCA were *not* happy.

Bowie was getting restless again, wanting to move on not only musically but also from Berlin itself. The feeling was exacerbated by the rise of neo-Nazi activity in his neighbourhood (his local Turkish cafe was attacked; Bowie quietly paid for repairs). Feeling that the welfare of his son was paramount, in the spring of 1979 he returned to America, taking a loft apartment with Schwab on 26th Street in Manhattan; Alomar and his wife lived on the same block. His time in Berlin, and the 'triptych' it inspired, left an indelible mark, though. 'Nothing else sounded like those albums. Nothing else came close,' he told *Uncut* proudly in 2001. 'If I never made another album it really wouldn't matter now, my complete being is within those three. They are my DNA.'

8

Scary Monsters
(and Superstardom)

I n February 1980 Bowie's divorce from Angie was
finalized. The settlement allotted her only around
$700,000 in alimony, over ten years, and banned her
from discussing their life with the media for the same
period. Bowie had custody of their son, Joe, to whom she
was allowed only limited access (he'd dropped the 'Zowie'
early on and would eventually settle on 'Duncan'). Intense
touring during the seventies had kept Bowie apart from
him for long stretches, something that he now sought to
redress. In the coming decade, he'd send Joe to the illustrious
Scottish boarding school Gordonstoun, although he took
care to make time for the two of them to be together, too.

Bowie was now healthier physically and financially, and
hungry to record again. When he joined up with the DAM
Trio and Tony Visconti at New York's Power Station in
February 1980, cerebral strategies and art for its own sake
were out; grooves and hit-making were triumphantly back.
He'd seduced Lou Reed's guitarist Chuck Hammer and his
Roland GR-300 guitar synth away for the sessions, just as
he'd spirited away Adrian Belew from Frank Zappa's band
for *Lodger*. The album would be completed at Visconti's Good

Earth Studios, where Pete Townshend and Robert Fripp contributed guitar parts. Fripp's, in particular, were special: screeching slabs of noise that, like Hammer's contributions, worked as texture.

Released on 12 September 1980, *Scary Monsters (And Super Creeps)* returned Bowie to No. 1 in the UK for the first time since *Diamond Dogs* in 1974 (in the USA, the album reached No. 12). Its deft mix of catchy melodies with freaky art noise and dance beats made a richly rewarding set, and for many it would be Bowie's last great album. It was also the first on which he so explicitly referenced his past, most obviously with the reappearance of Major Tom from 'Space Oddity' on 'Ashes to Ashes', a mesmerizing blend of play-ground singalong and spooky morality tale, with Hammer's 'Guitarchitecture' providing layers of synthesized texture. (The stop-start beat came from 'My Girl' by Madness, one of Joe's favourite bands.) 'Fashion' is almost as good, a satire of herd mentality in all its forms, featuring more left-field guitar aggression from Fripp. The sprightly 'Up the Hill Backwards' takes the paparazzi to task. Fripp dials it down for 'Teenage Wildlife', a slap at the way stars are built up, with echoes of "Heroes" and a terrifically mannered vocal. 'Scream Like a Baby' revisits the glowering totalitarianism of *Diamond Dogs* (as with about half of the album, it's a reworking of an earlier, abandoned track, in this case 'I Am a Laser' from 1974, earmarked for Ava Cherry's group the Astronettes). 'Because You're Young' offers advice to Bowie's neglected son. Bookending the set are two versions of 'It's No Game': the first edgy and swaggering, with Bowie at his vocal limits; the second crooning, more reflective.

Bowie-as-Pierrot on the sleeve was realized by the illustrator Edward Bell, although past Bowies were present, too. The shadow in the Brian Duffy photograph behind him echoes the singer's pose for *"Heroes"*, while the rear cover features glimpses of all three 'Berlin Trilogy' albums and *Aladdin Sane*. Appropriately, the clown costume, which evokes Lindsay Kemp and Bowie's piece *Pierrot in Turquoise* (1970), was created by Kemp's onetime designer Natasha Korniloff.

Through the theatrical and film impresario Michael White, Bowie had become aware of the nascent new romantic movement in Britain. Its key venue – Blitz – had started out as a Bowie night on Tuesdays in the seedy Billy's nightclub, beneath a brothel on Dean Street in Soho; the club's cloakroom attendant, Boy George, had been among the fans hanging around Haddon Hall in the early seventies, and cherished the memory of Angie telling him to fuck off. Eventually, the club moved to the larger Blitz wine bar in Covent Garden; Rusty Egan, who DJed there, built his set around Bowie and the German bands he'd admired. At White's suggestion, Bowie himself dropped in at Blitz, recruiting four of the regulars, including club founder Steve Strange, for the ground-breaking 'Ashes to Ashes' video, filmed on Hastings beach. Co-directed with David Mallet, it included innovative colouration techniques that turned the skies a brooding black, under which Bowie led his dourly garbed Blitz quartet along the sands in front of a bulldozer; later on, he receives a lecture from a mum figure. The results set a benchmark for the eighties music-video explosion.

Several leading lights of new romantic pop had been Bowie fans since *Ziggy Stardust*, so the transition from glam rock to glamorous pop was logical for them. Simon Le Bon of Duran Duran and Spandau Ballet's Tony Hadley both honed the epic, full-throated vocals that Bowie had brought to *"Heroes"* and *Lodger*, as did U2's Bono and Ian McCulloch of indie darlings Echo and the Bunnymen.[1] Like Joy Division, the artier synthpop outfit Japan (managed by Marc Bolan's former mentor Simon Napier-Bell) favoured the colder, fractured ambience of *Low*; at the scene's poppier fringes lay Steve Strange's Visage, whose haunting 'Fade to Grey' became a Top 10 hit in the UK. Martin Fry's ABC purveyed a lush, bright sound, but Bowie's Berlin period resonated strongly with them, too. 'Bowie was plugged into how my generation was feeling,' affirmed Fry. 'Alienated, nervous about the future, tense on amphetamines, saving up to buy synthesizers, paranoid and skint.'

For some contemporary rock bands and critics, synthesizers weren't 'real' instruments – but then Bowie had always given authenticity short shrift. Before the likes of himself and Roxy Music, there had been an implicit connection between singers and their material, as if they embodied it: 'A rock star didn't perform the songs, he *was* the songs,' as David Hepworth observes in his book *Uncommon People*. But Bowie was never about that, which made him less genuine in the eyes of many contemporary critics and music fans. With his whirlwind brain and ever-changing appetites, he was far closer to George Walden's definition of the dandy:

---

[1] Famously, in a move to transcend their worthy rock image, U2 recruited Brian Eno for *Achtung Baby*, recorded in Berlin's Hansa Tonstudio in 1991.

'In the dandyist philosophy impermanence alone endures … convictions and consistency are for dullards.'[2]

Bowie had seen Bernard Pomerance's play *The Elephant Man*, based on the life of the tragically deformed Joseph Merrick, directed by Jack Hofsiss, and considered it something he'd like to have attempted himself; doubtless the theme of a sensitive but isolated outsider chimed with him. Lo and behold, in February 1980, during the *Scary Monsters* sessions, Hofsiss contacted him to ask if he'd consider taking over the title role, since the lead actor was leaving. Bowie agreed, immersing himself in rigorous preparation and research, including a trip to the Royal London Hospital, where Merrick had lived and which still housed his skeleton and personal belongings. The play also gave Bowie the chance to use his skill at mime, not least in equipping his body to withstand the contortions that he had to maintain during the lengthy performance, and to convey nuances of character (he performed without make-up and clad only in a loincloth for much of the time). His performance won respect not only from theatre crowds and critics but also from the cast, who were impressed by his unstarry knuckling-down. The tour moved from Denver to Chicago and finally, in September, to New York. John Lennon, Yoko Ono and Iggy Pop were among the backstage well-wishers.

Lennon's comeback album *Double Fantasy* was released in November, breaking five years of recording silence. On 6 December he and Ono were interviewed by the BBC's

[2] See George Walden and Jules Barbey d'Aurevilly, *Who's a Dandy?* (London: Gibson Square Books, 2002).

Andy Peebles at the Hit Factory in New York, and towards
the end of the chat Peebles mentioned that Bowie had
commented on the lack of hassle he'd experienced in
New York. Lennon warmly concurred. 'I mean, people
will come up for an autograph, or say hi, but they won't
bug you, you know?' Two days later he was shot dead by
a deranged fan, and everything changed. Bowie was devastated – and scared. He completed most of the remaining
run, but suddenly New York didn't feel safe; there were
reports that Lennon's assassin, Mark David Chapman,
had been seeking him out, too. He retreated to his home
in Switzerland to take stock.

* * * * *

In the twilight years of his legal settlement with Tony
Defries, smaller and more diverse projects competed
for Bowie's interest. In 1981 he collaborated with
the disco pioneer Giorgio Moroder on the underrated 'Cat People (Putting out Fire)', the title track
from Paul Schrader's take on Jacques Tourneur's
noir horror from 1942, on which he delivers
a finely measured vocal. It was recorded at Mountain
Studios at Montreux, the *Lodger* studio and the site
for another fruitful pairing, when Bowie met Queen,
who were recording their *Hot Space* LP. Lyrically driven
by Bowie (witness its anxious undercurrents), 'Under
Pressure' gave him his third UK No. 1 and Queen their
second. It also gave him the opportunity to quiz Queen's
singer Freddie Mercury about their label, EMI.

The following year marked another memorable acting outing for Bowie, in a BBC adaptation of Bertolt Brecht's 1918 play *Baal* – the story of a narcissistic, amoral, sexually promiscuous, banjo-playing young poet – directed by Alan Clarke. Bowie was familiar with the subjects of Weimar-era Germany and Brecht's oeuvre, and throughout filming he was engaged and cooperative. Not only was he able to make incisive and pertinent comments on the music, but also his knowledge of Expressionist art contributed to the staging of the play. He returned to Berlin to cut a five-track EP of Brecht's songs, produced by Tony Visconti, with the leading Brecht interpreter Dominic Muldowney. It was an artistic triumph, as Muldowney later attested, paying tribute to Bowie's exceptional phrasing, 'an absolute tutorial in how to paint a text'. These recordings, made at Hansa Studio 2 over a couple of days, were to be Bowie's last in the city, and the EP would be his last release for RCA.

In early 1982 Bowie took on another film role, that of Major Jack Celliers, an internee in a Japanese prisoner-of-war camp in Nagisa Oshima's *Merry Christmas, Mr Lawrence*. The electronic pop pioneer Ryuichi Sakamoto, who'd never acted before, played the camp's commander, Captain Yonoi, and the homosexual undertones of Yonoi's fascination with Celliers is one of the movie's major themes. Oshima had become convinced of Bowie's potential when he saw him during the New York run of *The Elephant Man*, and the singer turned in another commendable performance, one praised by Janet Maslin of the *New York Times* as 'mercurial and arresting … The demands of his role may sometimes be improbable and elaborate, but Mr Bowie fills them in a remarkably plain and direct way.' The movie spawned an intriguing soundtrack by Sakamoto, while the title track provided a sparkling UK Top 20 hit single in 'Forbidden Colours'. Its singer, David Sylvian, formerly of the art-rock outfit Japan, owed a clear debt to Bowie in his vocal mannerisms and look, as did Peter Murphy of Bauhaus, who had scored a UK hit in 1982 with an identikit cover of 'Ziggy Stardust'. Bauhaus also appeared at the start of Bowie's next film, Tony Scott's vampire flick *The Hunger* (1983), performing their none-more-goth single 'Bela Lugosi's Dead'. His son, Joe, accompanied Bowie on set, an experience that fostered a burgeoning interest in film and a long-standing friendship with the director. Having been expelled from Gordonstoun for napping in his English A-Level exam, he continued his education at Wooster, a liberal-arts college in Ohio, where he adopted the name Duncan. In 1999 Bowie took him on set to see Scott's TV adaptation of *The Hunger*, rekindling their friendship. Duncan went on to enrol at the London Film School and would serve as a camera operator for Scott before, via commercials and music videos, he began directing his own short films.

In 1982 Bowie bought a luxurious new home in Switzerland, the Château du Signal in Lausanne, but after *Merry Christmas, Mr Lawrence* wrapped, he began to spend more time in New York again, accompanied by bodyguards. That autumn he bumped into Nile Rodgers at Continental, an after-hours club. Rodgers had been the architect, with bassist Bernard Edwards, of Chic's elegant disco hits, including – in 'Le Freak' – what was until then Atlantic Records' biggest-selling single. (Improbably, his band had also supported the Stooges.) The two had gone on to sprinkle production gold dust on hits for Sister Sledge and Diana Ross, but of late Rodgers had suffered a string of flops. Still, he was a proven hit-maker, and Bowie now wanted a hit. For inspiration, he showed Rodgers a photograph of Little Richard in a red suit, stepping into a bright red Cadillac. The vibe: dancefloor-friendly pop, drawing on vintage rock 'n' roll and R&B but with a contemporary twist; brass that recalled Richard's great primal fifties hits and the big bands of the thirties and forties. The goal: a commercial-sounding album that would garner Bowie a generous new record deal.

* * * * *

Released on 14 April 1983, *Let's Dance* is often cited as the album on which Bowie stifled his artistic instincts to go flat out for commercial success. With expectations raised after *Scary Monsters*, the album went platinum on both sides of the Atlantic, shifting about 10 million copies – making it comfortably his bestselling LP – and producing a handful of huge hit singles. On its promise, EMI America had signed Bowie for around $17 million on 27 January 1983. Like a spurned ex-lover, RCA got in on the act by re-releasing Bowie's back catalogue at a budget price, resulting in his albums simultaneously holding 10 places in the UK Top 100.

In retrospect, *Let's Dance* is a mixed bag. It's hard to argue with the brassy swagger of 'Let's Dance' (a No. 1 in both the UK and the USA), highlighted by a terrific solo from Stevie Ray Vaughan, whose band Bowie had met at Montreux Jazz Festival the previous year, and ascending harmonies straight out of 'Twist and Shout'. Even then, older, fretful Bowie haunts the lyrics. Musically, 'Modern Love' – another huge hit – is a punchy delight, driven on by snappy call-and-response backing vocals, although again the words suggest a narrator perpetually frustrated in his search for meaning in life. 'China Girl', from Iggy Pop's *The Idiot*, takes the subject of a relationship (based on Iggy's fling with Kuelan Nguyen, a Vietnamese girl he'd met at the Château d'Hérouville) and works in sinister overtones of cultural imperialism and atrocities, hence the reference to swastikas. Rodgers adds light to Bowie's version, stamping the start with a straightforwardly Asian-sounding riff adapted from Rufus's 'Sweet Thing', which he'd covered in the Big Apple Band, his pre-Chic outfit, and a gently descending line of backing vocals.

As with *The Lodger*, some songs revisit older material ('China Girl' and 'Cat People [Putting out Fire]'). 'Shake It' is faceless and empty; 'Without You' is notable largely for the presence of Rodgers's musical partners in Chic, Bernard Edwards and drummer Tony Thompson. The nigh-on obligatory cover ('Criminal World' by Metro) is more diverting, a reworking of an obscure track from 1976 with bisexual undercurrents, although Bowie expunges the more explicit implications. At the time, however, the set's success was absolute. It would even be nominated for Album of the Year at the Grammys, eventually losing out to Michael Jackson's all-conquering *Thriller*.

Bowie had shown his mastery of video with 'Ashes to Ashes' and capitalized on it with his new album, once again recruiting Mallet. Shot in Australia, 'Let's Dance' portrayed rampant white capitalist consumerism; young Aborigines are landed with Sisyphean tasks, a shorthand for their race's cultural disempowerment. Elsewhere, 'China Girl' references Deborah Kerr and Burt Lancaster's love 'n' surf scene in 1953's *From Here to Eternity*, adding an anti-racist twist. A bare-buttocked Bowie enjoys close congress with his co-star (and, briefly, lover) Geeling Ng; any attendant controversy harmed sales not one whit, and the video picked up an MTV award for Best Male Video.

Along with the simpler, chart-friendly sound came a fresh, easily accessible look, unveiled at a press conference at Claridge's hotel in London on 17 March. This incarnation of Bowie was tanned, with bleached blond hair, a trim, besuited frame (check out boxer Dave on the album's cover) and a ready laugh, the epitome of a healthy, uncomplicated pop star for the times. Indeed, something about that buoyant golden 'do summoned up the David Jones who'd played sax for the Kon-Rads. On the album's supporting seven-month *Serious Moonlight* world tour, he played 96 dates in 15 countries, shifting more than 2.5 million tickets in his most successful concerts to date. And if he still wasn't drug-free ('I was not in great shape to accept success at any level,' he reflected ruefully to *Arena* magazine in 1993), his dabbling was more restrained.

Bowie had, rather quickly, become a conventional star, and in a rather old-fashioned way, too, with chart successes backed up by a movie career. Had the 'generalist' at last become an all-round entertainer, the mutual goal of those very different ex-managers Kenneth Pitt and Tony Defries? In April 1983, to *NME*, he expressed his hope that he was abandoning the 'nihilistic quality which was so much part of my early music', partly out of paternal responsibility ('The one most enjoyable and hope-giving quality of my life over the past four or five years is my son'). By May he was telling *Rolling Stone* that his public coming-out 11 years earlier had been the act of a young, naive artist who had simply been experimenting.

If *Let's Dance* significantly boosted Bowie's finances, its sheen and calculation compromised his artistry. Its polished perfection flew in the face of his inherent openness to failure. ('If I haven't made three good mistakes in a week, then I'm not worth anything,' he'd told *NME* in 1977. 'You only learn from mistakes'.) He once credited his half-brother Terry as his inspiration for 'not being drawn to the tyranny of the mainstream'. Now, for perhaps the first time since the mid-sixties, he'd written music to please others – a label he was courting; the broader record-buying public – rather than himself. Where was the mystery and risk-taking that had been his practice for so long? It was clear what he'd gained, but what had he lost?

9

Losing the Muse

Many iconic artists found the eighties difficult to navigate. Stevie Wonder, one of Bowie's few rivals as a game-changer in the seventies, dramatically lost his mojo after *Hotter Than July* in 1980. In his autobiography, Bob Dylan confessed to feeling lost by 1987: 'A folk-rock relic, a wordsmith from bygone days, a fictitious head of state from a place nobody knows.' That it should happen to David Bowie, though, felt particularly wrong. His artistic compass had unfailingly led him into fresh, uncharted territories. His influence had extended beyond pop into culture at large, arguably more so than anyone since the Beatles. And, while the Fabs had retired from live performance in 1966 to become a studio band, Bowie had toured audaciously ambitious albums, such as *Diamond Dogs* and *Station to Station*, to widespread acclaim.

But the success of *Let's Dance*, and the pressure to repeat it, derailed Bowie's maverick instincts. Some five months after his *Serious Moonlight* world tour, he was in Le Studio in Morin-Heights, Canada, to record *Tonight*. Despite platinum sales and an initially positive reception (*NME*'s Charles Shaar Murray praised its 'dizzying variety of mood and technique'), it sounds like *Let's Dance*'s poor relation. Bowie never gelled with the producer, Derek Bramble, and the engineer Hugh Padgham eventually took over. Possibly because there'd been little time to work up new material, the album leans even more heavily on co-writes and covers than its predecessor, including a pointless remake of the Beach Boys' 'God Only Knows'. Iggy Pop contributes to five tracks, including *Lust For Life*'s 'Neighbourhood Threat' and 'Tonight'. The latter is reimagined as an anonymous reggaefied duet with Tina Turner, lacking the opening narration from Iggy's original, which provides the graphic context; it's sung to a lover who is overdosing, but Bowie told Murray that that 'seemed not part of my vocabulary'. The catchy 'Blue Jean' was a No. 6 UK hit, while Julien Temple's accompanying 22-minute video, in which Bowie plays both the rock star Screamin' Lord Byron and an ordinary Ernie in the crowd, won a Grammy. But despite the pop sheen, the content flags. Even the Gilbert and George-style sleeve seems somewhat thrown together.

Padgham had also worked with the Police, but on *Tonight* the touches of white reggae – a notoriously difficult genre to pull off – fail to convince. The gated reverb on the drums, which the producer later famously employed on Phil Collins's solo albums (exhibit A: 'Something in the Air'), often feels like an aural slap in the face. Best of the bunch is 'Loving the Alien', an intriguing if flawed meditation on organized religion and its damaging effects, from the Crusades to the present, that Bowie valued and spent considerable time on. Those seeking the allusive, intriguing Bowie who'd abruptly gone AWOL would have found a trace of him in the haunting 'This Is Not America', a collaboration with the Pat Metheny Group for the soundtrack of John Schlesinger's spy drama *The Falcon and the Snowman* (1985).

In January 1985 Bowie's troubled half-brother finally achieved peace. After an earlier failed attempt at suicide by leaping from a window, Terry Burns ended his life on the tracks at Coulsdon South railway station. Bowie had faced criticism from within his own family for supposedly neglecting Terry during much of the preceding decade, although he'd visited him after the unsuccessful suicide bid. But it's undeniable that his death devastated the singer. He didn't attend the funeral, but sent red roses along with a note that read 'You've seen more things than we could imagine but all these moments will be lost, like tears washed away by the rain. God bless you – David.'

The mid-eighties saw Bowie admirably embrace a string of different projects, the only caveat being that they prevented him from devoting time and energy to producing another worthwhile album. In July 1985 he put in a whole-hearted performance at Wembley Stadium for Live Aid, the charity concert broadcast globally, with a sister event in Philadelphia. "Heroes" gave the event the euphoric can-do spirit it deserved. An overcooked cover of Martha and the Vandellas' sublime 'Dancing in the Street' with his erstwhile rival Mick Jagger raised further funds for the cause and made UK No. 1. At least David Mallet's video of the two attempting to out-dance and out-camp each other was fun.

Bowie's turn as Jareth the Goblin King in Jim Henson's kids' fantasy movie *Labyrinth* (1986), to which he also contributed a soundtrack, introduced him to a young generation. (His son worked on making the puppets, an early sign of his interest in filmmaking.) Sporting a very of-its-decade fright wig and a bulging codpiece that became a talking point in its own right, his performance flummoxed many critics (and the songs were terrible). But it went some way to giving the movie its cult allure, as Jareth's blend of sexuality and malevolence made him an ambivalent figure to the movie's heroine, Sarah (Jennifer Connelly), a girl on the cusp of adulthood. The following year Bowie would add to his eclectic actor's CV with a worthy cameo as Pilate in Martin Scorsese's *The Last Temptation of Christ*.

Colin MacInnes's novel *Absolute Beginners*, the tale of a gay teenager finding his way in late fifties Notting Hill – then experiencing the birth pains of multiculturalism and a new British youth culture – must have appealed to the mod in Bowie. He turned out a cracking title track, a disarmingly open-hearted lyric with soaring vocal that deservedly hit UK No. 2 and which he credited as 'the best of very few love songs that I've written'. It rather outshone his brief appearance in the movie as advertising mogul Vendice Partners for the song-and-dance routine 'That's Motivation'. Unfortunately, despite its good intentions – to add a dash of brio and vitality to the British film industry – the film bombed. Still, Bowie himself had much to celebrate: he was in good health and financially buoyant, with a scattering of luxurious properties across the globe, ranging from the 14-room Château du Signal in Switzerland to his apartment in the sought-after Kincoppal block in Sydney's Elizabeth Bay. A few years later he had the extraordinary Balinese-style holiday home 'Mandalay' created for him in Mustique.

Once again Bowie turned his attention back to Iggy, co-producing his set *Blah-Blah-Blah* in 1986, a belated hit album featuring the former Stooge's first hit single in a cover of Johnny O'Keefe's 'Wild One', and co-writing several tracks, notably 'Shades'. But the following year, he plumbed a new nadir with *Never Let Me Down*. The album at least attempted to break out of the main-stream straitjacket, with a sound refocused on hard-edged rock guitar, artier conceits ('Glass Spider') and ten new compositions. But it was over-rehearsed and overproduced; the intrusive eighties drums were a particularly nagging distraction, while the various attempts at social commentary fail to cohere or convince (something they shared with the album's sleeve). The better tracks – 'Time Will Crawl' and the title track (with its curious Lennon-esque vocal), a heartfelt tribute to Coco Schwab – make the lack of quality elsewhere even more glaring. In the post-mortems, Bowie admitted he'd relinquished control ('I let go and it became very soft musically, which wasn't the way I would have done it if I had been more involved'), just as he'd downplayed his input on *Let's Dance* and *Tonight*.

Nevertheless, the subsequent *Glass Spider* stadium tour grossed $50 million-plus and comfortably topped 'Serious Moonlight' in ticket sales. But, while hugely ambitious, with a renewed emphasis on theatricality, the concerts epitomized how unsure of himself David Bowie now was. On stage, he was competing for attention with live dancers choreographed by Toni Basil, who'd worked on the *Diamond Dogs* tour, an outing whose theatricality Bowie was keen to pursue via the theme of rock stars and their public perception. Wireless technology enabled him to cover vast areas of the stage, making for a more physical performance along the lines of Madonna's demanding athleticism. Perhaps in an effort to stand out, he sported a vivid red single-breasted suit, shirt and shoes, topped off by a gravity-defying mullet.

Early on, all but two of the tracks from *Never Let Me Down* were aired, but in time older hits replaced the newer material, something that Bowie had initially been dead against. The set was dominated by an 18-metre-tall spider with tubular legs that changed colour but were seen to best effect only in darkness. It was too large for some arenas, so a scaled-down model had to be built. Complex vocal interplay between himself and the dancers (partly live, partly taped) could be frustrated by inclement weather at open-air venues. And a coffer-lining sponsorship deal with Pepsi did little for his artistic credibility.

One green shoot appeared in the form of Reeves Gabrels, whose wife, Sara Terry, had worked on press for the *Glass Spider* tour and had passed the singer a tape of her husband's work. Gabrels was a Berklee-trained guitarist who'd also studied art and was alive to the sculptural possibilities of guitar noise. In June 1988 Bowie took part in a brief dance routine in a fundraiser for the Institute of Contemporary Arts, London, at the city's Dominion Theatre, with Louise Lecavalier of the avant-garde Quebec dance company La La La Human Steps. In a trio that also included Erdal Kızılçay, a multi-instrumentalist who'd

David Bowie

worked on *Never Let Me Down*, Gabrels provided an
intense, brutal take on *Lodger*'s 'Look Back in Anger' to
accompany the performance. Gabrels and Bowie reconvened in Switzerland, where the former encouraged Bowie
simply to make the music he wanted to make – and hang
EMI. Recruiting Tony and Hunt Sales, formerly of Iggy
Pop's band, and (temporarily) second guitarist Tony
Armstrong, they dubbed themselves Tin Machine after one
of their songs and began working up ideas in Montreux,
continuing at Compass Point studios in Nassau. With
spontaneity and immediacy as yardsticks, they honed
a bullish, guitar-orientated sound that referenced contemporary noise merchants such as Sonic Youth and Pixies.

Much critical opprobrium has been dumped on it since,
but Tin Machine was conceived as a chance for Bowie to
share responsibility with others instead of shouldering it
all himself, although whether that was feasible in practice
is another matter. (In late 1972, when he was still Ziggy,
he'd told Mott the Hoople's Ian Hunter that you could
never have a truly democratic band.) For its producer, Tim
Palmer, Tin Machine's eponymous debut album of 1989
(a UK No. 3 hit) was grunge before its time, although others
heard a return to the hard-rock heyday of Led Zeppelin
and Cream. Early upbeat reviews praised mindful lyrics
that addressed the rise of neo-Nazis and inner-city drug
epidemics, but thereafter came sliding sales and a poorly
received follow-up, released on Victory as EMI shunned it.[1]

---

[1] Bowie remained adamant that the experience was positive. He told *NME*
in 1993: 'Working with Tin Machine was a confidence-builder, because
I lost my confidence during the eighties.'

126

Beginning in 1989, Rykodisc began re-releasing Bowie's RCA back catalogue in superbly remastered CD versions that included rare tracks. At the same time an excellent box set, *Sound + Vision*, appeared; incorporating out-takes, demo versions and live recordings, it was rapturously received, and won a Grammy for Best Album Package. Its success spawned what Bowie claimed, at the time, would be his only 'greatest hits' tour. *Sound + Vision*, which kicked off in January 1990, incorporated 108 performances across 27 countries. The stage set harked back to the starkly lit 'Brechtian' approach of the *Station to Station* dates, while on some dates members of La La La Human Steps performed on stage. The set also featured a diaphanous gauze screen on to which videos were projected, blocking off most of the band (save for the newly recruited guitarist Adrian Belew), which pissed them off royally. The fans, though, were delighted; the tour grossed some $20 million and restored much of the goodwill lost by the *Glass Spider* debacle. A compilation in 1990, *ChangesBowie*, gave the singer his first UK No. 1 since 1984.

Bowie's appearance at the Freddie Mercury Tribute Concert at Wembley Stadium on 20 April 1992 is remembered now not so much for his version of 'Under Pressure' with Annie Lennox deputizing for Mercury, nor even for his final reunion with a visibly ailing Mick Ronson on 'All the Young Dudes' and "Heroes", as for the moment he dropped to his knees and recited the Lord's Prayer. Was this the man who had once railed against organized religion, telling Charles Shaar Murray in 1984 that 'It's extraordinary considering all the mistranslations in the Bible that our lives are being navigated by this misinformation, and that so many people have died because of it'?

Within four days Bowie was married. He'd met his bride, the supermodel Iman Mohamed Abdulmajid, through a mutual friend in October 1990 and had fallen for her immediately, revealing later that 'I was naming the children the night we met ... I knew that she was for me; it was absolutely immediate.' The low-key wedding took place in Lausanne; two months later a second ceremony took place in Florence, where the congregation was joined by celeb-friend-with-deep-pockets *Hello!* magazine. The couple planned to settle in Los Angeles, an intriguing choice given Bowie's history there. But on arrival they found themselves confined to their hotel: they'd flown in on the day that riots kicked off following the acquittal of LAPD officers accused of beating the African-American construction worker Rodney King. The newly-weds plumped for New York instead.

The success of the Rykodisc reissue campaign, alongside the *Sound + Vision* box set and tour, had reaffirmed Bowie's status, and the Dame himself now seemed more at ease with his past.[2] *Black Tie, White Noise* (1993), his first solo album for the nineties, returned Bowie to the UK No. 1 spot and Nile Rodgers to the producer's seat. Certainly there are highs, from the ebullient cover of the

---

[2] The epithet was coined by the *Smash Hits* writer Tom Hibbert in response to the twin pratfalls of the *Never Let Me Down* album and the attendant *Glass Spider* tour: 'If Dame David Bowie is such a bleeding chameleon, why, pray, can't he change into something more exciting than the skin of an ageing rock plodder?'

Walker Brothers' 'Nite Flights' to the skittery 'Jump They Say' (a UK No. 9, it was inspired partly by the shock of Terry Burns's suicide and Bowie's feelings towards him) and 'You've Been Around', written with Reeves Gabrels for Tin Machine, on which a backing vocal references his classic 'Changes' from 1971. Elsewhere, 'Black Tie, White Noise' revisits Bowie's experience of the Los Angeles riots the previous year. Aside from 'Looking for Lester', on which he solos on sax alongside his namesake the jazz trumpeter Lester Bowie, that's pretty much the best of it. The gushing 'The Wedding' harks back to the nuptials, while a cover of Cream's 'I Feel Free' features a solo from Ronson, who'd also produced 'I Know It's Gonna Happen Someday' on Morrissey's acclaimed set *Your Arsenal* the previous year; here, Bowie's high-camp performance is couched in glam-rock reverb.[3]

At the time, Britain's hottest new band was Suede, whose crunchy guitars and yelped vocals had strong glam-rock roots. In March 1993, with both *Black Tie, White Noise* and Suede's eponymous debut album shortly to be released, *NME* convened a co-interview between the band's singer Brett Anderson and the Dame. For good measure, Bowie brought along a contact sheet of photos from an earlier celebrated head-to-head, his meeting with William Burroughs for *Rolling Stone* in 1974, and wore a fedora and suit, as Burroughs had. Bowie told Anderson that Suede were 'far nearer Roxy Music' than himself. And when Anderson,

---

[3] Ronson died from liver cancer on 23 April 1993. Bowie didn't appear at a tribute concert at Hammersmith Odeon for the guitarist, for reasons that remain unclear.

defending his band against accusations of hype, insisted that 'I'd never wanna appear like a media fabrication', Bowie coolly countered: 'Ah, therein lies the difference … I may not have had any real understanding of why or how, but what I was doing was a fabrication.'

Hanif Kureishi's semi-autobiographical 1990 novel *The Buddha of Suburbia* was very much Bowie territory, with its themes of bisexuality and the frustration of growing up on the fringes of city life. Both men were ex-Bromleyites, a fact that came up frequently when Kureishi conducted a Q&A with Bowie for the US *Interview* magazine in early 1993. It was entirely fitting, then, that Bowie, working with Erdal Kızılçay at Mountain Studios, should supply the title track for a BBC2 adaptation three years later, although on the resulting 'soundtrack' album only The Buddha of Suburbia' itself – a nod to his teenage years, which bookends the set and alludes to 'All the Madmen' – remained from the TV series. For the rest, Bowie took brief musical themes and looped them or slowed them down, creating a new platform for further textural layering. Noting only the key and length of a track, he'd bring all the faders down save for the percussion, then add more musical elements before pushing up the faders once more. 'A number of clashes would make themselves evident,' he observed in the sleeve notes, with a scientist's detachment. 'The more dangerous or attractive ones would then be isolated and repeated.' Underrated, underpromoted and outsold heavily by his *Singles Collection* at the time, the album nonetheless revealed Bowie's avant-garde impulses to be alive and well. Not since *"Heroes"* had he produced such intriguing instrumentals, from the soothing waves of 'The Mysteries' to the eerie, hissing 'Ian Fish, UK Heir' (an anagram of Kureishi's name).

Bowie's notes acknowledged the album's retrospective tone, and in a 'personal memory stock' for the set he listed 'Kraftwerk', 'Blues Clubs Soho', 'Unter de Linden [sic]', 'Travels thru Russia' and 'Brücke Museum in Berlin'. He also paid homage to Brian Eno, who hadn't been involved in this project but would be all over the next.

10

Art-house Rules

With the album *1. Outside*, released in September 1995, David Bowie and Brian Eno reconvened their self-titled 'school of pretension' for what was intended as the first instalment of a five-LP series concerning art and murder, and death as art. When they set up shop at Montreux Studios in March 1994, high-concept was very much to the fore. During the sessions, Bowie sometimes painted at an easel. The musicians were each given a card bearing a cryptic text by Eno: 'You are a disgruntled ex-member of a South African rock band. Play the notes you were not allowed to play'. Day-long jams provided some 30 hours of raw material, and to anchor it, Bowie evolved a story about art, ritual and homicide in a suburban Oxford Town, inventing characters along the way: Adler, of the Art-Crime Inc. office; Baby Grace Blue, the 14-year-old victim, whose dismembered body is left outside the town's 'Museum of Modern Parts'; and the mysterious Artist/Minotaur. He also added bridging monologues in character. It all made for wilfully indulgent art and an uncommercial 75-minute playing time.

Bin the intellectual scaffolding, and what do you get? Edgy, industrial 'The Heart's Filthy Lesson', heard over the closing credits of the film *Se7en* that year, and the giddy rush of 'Hallo Spaceboy'. A disco-flavoured remix of the latter by the Pet

Shop Boys provided a UK No. 12 hit. Their *Top of the* Pops performance presented the latest Bowie, who resembled a hip young priest in stilettos. 'We Prick You' and 'I'm Deranged' hint at the jungle beats that would enliven his next album, and 'Thru These Architect's Eyes' is highlighted by a strong vocal and Mike Garson's piano interventions. 'A Small Plot of Land' visits the troubled territories scoped out by Scott Walker from the late seventies onwards. Some critics felt that the material sagged under the weight of all that pretension, but most welcomed its ambition. Remarkably, it charted well, too, hitting No. 8 in the UK and No. 21 Stateside.

1. Outside had shown Bowie venturing into more chal-lenging areas of rock and dance music than his peers dared. Nine Inch Nails (who supported him on the US leg of the accompanying tour, their respective sets segueing into each other) and Underworld were other touchstones. Morrissey, the initial support act on the UK tour, was an ardent glam fan, but bridled at the suggestion that their sets should overlap, and lasted only ten dates. Placebo replaced him, and the band also appeared at Bowie's fiftieth birthday celebrations at Madison Square Garden, an event dominated by younger artists (Pixies' Black Francis, the Smashing Pumpkins' Billy Corgan, the Foo Fighters). Only Lou Reed offered a line back to Bowie's stellar seventies.

The major talking point about *Earthling* (1997) was its use of the helter-skelter rhythms of jungle (by then better known as drum 'n' bass), born in British clubs at the start of the decade and with pioneers including Goldie, LTJ Bukem and Rebel MC. As with Bowie's adoption of the aggressive industrial sounds of bands such as Nine Inch Nails, this again prompted accusations of filching slightly outdated musical trends. The taster 'Telling Lies' (the first download single by an artist of Bowie's stature, released nearly a decade before iTunes and shifting 300,000-plus downloads) blended breakneck beats with goth austerity, not altogether successfully. The quirky pop charm of 'Little Wonder' just about stays the course with its scuttling rhythms, until the metal-style drop to half-speed. The thumping 'Seven Years in Tibet' nods to Bowie's interest in both Buddhism and Tibet's treatment by China. At its worst, *Earthling* welds pell-mell beats and crunching guitars on to songs that would do equally well, if not better, without them. But even if drum 'n' bass no longer quite represented the shock of the new, there's no doubting Bowie's enthusiasm for the genre: 'I guess it's how rock was for the generation behind me, when it kicked in around '56 and everyone thought, "What is THAT?!!"' he enthused to *NME* in early 1997, also comparing its impact on him to his first experience of the Who.

Chief among Bowie's extra-musical interests were Bowie Bonds, an innovative concept whereby the singer offered future royalties to his back catalogue for a period of ten years as an 'asset backing', raising a reported $55 million. He used the money partly to pay British tax and partly, more pressingly, to secure the full rights and outright ownership of the masters of his recordings up to 1982 from his former manager Tony Defries. Predictably, he was also enthusiastic about the creative potential of the internet, a young Wild West whose pitfalls and dangers were not yet apparent. He delighted in the opportunity for exchanges between artist and fan, to provide up-to-the-second updates of works in progress and the potential for artistic cross-pollination. By 1998 he had a pair of websites up and running. The ISP BowieNet launched on 1 September that year, offering downloadable rarities, his own web diary and chat rooms (to which he sometimes contributed, anonymously) as well as the chance to live-stream concerts.

Bowie's next album, *'hours...'* (1999), proved an ultimately frustrating set. It largely dials down the harsher textures of its two predecessors for something slower and more intimate, but – although it hit UK No. 5 – the songs generally struggle to engage. Still, the standout 'Thursday's Child' is an understated charmer and provided a UK No. 16 hit, and 'Brilliant Tree', on which Bowie plays *koto* for the first time on record since 'Moss Garden' on *"Heroes"* in 1977, is a brief but evocative instrumental. The mix-and-match cover finds a floppy-haired Bowie cradling the head of his goateed *Earthling* self, framed by bitty typography and barcodes; like all his worst sleeves, it seems overthought.

Bowie had once claimed that the *Sound + Vision* tour in 1990 would be his last greatest-hits outing, but you can't keep a good back catalogue down. He proved as much with his celebrated closing set at Glastonbury festival on 25 June 2000. Decked out in an Alexander McQueen frock coat and sporting floppy locks, he charmed the crowd for two hours. The following month he reconvened with Tony Visconti for work on the mooted album *Toy*, intended to feature reworkings of some of his sixties songs alongside a handful of newer compositions. (They broke off in August after the much-hoped-for birth of Bowie's daughter, Alexandria 'Lexi' Zahra Jones.) One of the strongest tracks was 'Shadow Man', an unreleased song from the *Ziggy Stardust* sessions recast as a plaintive show-stopper. Scheduling problems with his label, Virgin, scuppered the release of the album, although tracks were leaked online, but eventually sessions for a new album ended up taking priority.

That album was 2002's *Heathen* (UK No. 5, US No. 14), a decent set recorded at Allaire Studios in the Catskill Mountains, New York State, with Visconti once more at the helm. 'Afraid' and 'Uncle Floyd' (now the poignant lament 'Slip Away'), both mooted for *Toy*, finally got their official release. Widescreen epics ('Slow Burn', a son of "Heroes") sit alongside the childlike 'A Better Future' and 'Everyone Says "Hi"', a surprisingly straightforward warm duvet of affection for a departing loved one that made the UK Top 20. Elsewhere, there are inspired covers of 'Cactus' from Pixies' visceral debut *Surfer Rosa*, Neil Young's 'I've Been Waiting for You' and 'I Took a Trip on a Gemini Spaceship', a single from 1968 by the Legendary Stardust Cowboy. Overall, it felt as if Bowie were taking stock – of family, contemporary life, growing older, death. The cover, by Jonathan Barnbrook, is one of Bowie's finest, a noirish nod to Man Ray that casts the singer as a glazed-eyed alien.

By now Bowie had taken up more-or-less permanent residence in New York, prompted by what he saw as the invasive press attention he attracted in London, and his public appearances gradually tapered off as family responsibilities took precedence. Exceptions included the Tibet House Concert at Carnegie Hall in February 2001. During the Concert for New York City at Madison Square Garden that October, in the wake of the 9/11 tragedies, he delivered a pared-down take on Simon and Garfunkel's 'America', accompanying himself on an Omnichord, and then an emotive full-band run-through of "Heroes". Two months later he had a more personal loss to confront when his mother's death was announced on 2 April. Familiar faces at the funeral service included the loyal Kenneth Pitt, who had kept in touch with Bowie's family. Bowie was back in his birth city again for the Meltdown festival in 2002 at the Royal Festival Hall, which he curated. He performed *Low* and *Heathen* in their entirety, leaving the audience exhilarated if exhausted. And few could have anticipated a set by the Legendary Stardust Cowboy.

The nineties had seen David Bowie rediscovering his focus; now he had stability in his home life and ownership of his back catalogue, and the hunger to push on that had always characterized his best work had returned. He'd even cut down on the cigarettes. By the start of 2003 he and Visconti were working on *Heathen*'s follow-up. When it arrived, encased in a hotchpotch anime-esque cover, *Reality* continued the upward trend maintained by *Heathen*; it's infused with something of the sound of *Scary Monsters* and the ambience of New York City, in all its high-strung positivity. 'Never Get Old' drops lyrical and musical references to his past work. Musings on wasted chances, ageing and death recur. Will the frustrated wife in 'She'll Drive the Big Car' plunge her vehicle into the Hudson River or not? (Either way, it's a scorcher of a track, on which Bowie revisits the falsetto and harmonies of *Young Americans*.) Lou Reed praised 'The Loneliest Guy' as one of Bowie's finest lyrics. Best of all, though, is the elegant closer, 'Bring Me the Disco King', a cool reflection on mortality set to smoky jazz, with Mike Garson on sparkling form.

Kicking off in October 2003, Bowie's *A Reality Tour* would be his largest and most demanding for half a decade, producing the highest-grossing concerts of 2004. Before long, though, it became apparent that its demands, in tandem with the lifestyle choices he'd made in the decades beforehand, were catching up with him. Dates were cancelled or rescheduled as he battled with laryngitis and then flu. Bizarrely, at a gig in Oslo, Norway, on 18 June 2004, a lollipop thrown from the crowd became momentarily stuck in his left eye. More seriously, a few days later, in Prague, he had to curtail his set after suffering from shoulder pains. Two days after that, after playing a festival in Scheessel, Germany, he collapsed. He'd actually been suffering from a blocked coronary artery, necessitating an emergency angioplasty operation and the fitting of stents. The rest of the tour was cancelled.

David Bowie stepped back. Not until 8 September 2005 did he reappear in public, for the Hurricane Katrina 'Fashion Rocks' benefit concert. There was a fragility in his rendering of 'Life on Mars?', dropped a full six semitones to accommodate his now reduced vocal range, and in his physical appearance. The following year the Grammys bestowed a lifetime achievement award on him and he appeared in Christopher Nolan's thriller *The Prestige* looking heavier and, finally, more like his age. His performance as the inventor Nikola Tesla was an underrated gem and, perhaps, a reminder that in the past he'd taken on acting roles as a break from the intensity of music-making by allowing someone else to direct him, or to close the door on a creative period. There would be a memorable cameo on the BBC/HBO show *Extras*, delivering the taunting 'Little Fat Man' to Ricky

Gervais, whom he befriended. But his appearance alongside Alicia Keys at another benefit concert, the Black Ball on 9 November, became his last high-profile performance.

Bowie retreated to his apartment at 285 Lafayette Street, New York, spending time with Lexi and in his expansive library, or strolling through Washington Square Park. He might drop in to Bottega Falai, a few doors down, for a prosciutto di Parma sandwich and cappuccino, or browse at favourite bookshops such as McNally Jackson or The Strand on Broadway. A rare public outing came in 2009, for the premiere of the science-fiction film *Moon*, the remarkable, BAFTA award-winning directorial debut by his son, Duncan Jones. Its core themes of anxiety, isolation and multiple selves had long been his father's stock-in-trade.

* * * * *

Even the closest Bowie observers found themselves wrong-footed when, on 8 January 2013 – his 66th birthday – the singer's website announced a new album to appear in March, and posted the video for its first single: 'Where Are We Now?' He had stage-managed his return, just as he'd managed his 'retirement' in 1973 and the retreat to Berlin. Only around 20 people were aware that Bowie and Visconti had been crafting his 24th album in a small New York studio for the previous two years, with the musicians who'd appeared on *Reality*.

The song was the unlikeliest of comebacks, a muted, melancholy reflection on Bowie's Berlin days, delivered in a voice that sounded older, even tremulous. It made No. 6 in the UK, his biggest hit since 'Absolute Beginners' in 1986.

The accompanying video, directed by Tony Oursler, featured Bowie in a T-shirt bearing the legend 'Song of Norway', the musical that had taken Hermione Farthingale away from him all those golden years ago. The sleeve of *The Next Day* boldly reappropriated the *"Heroes"* cover, its centre now obliterated by a white square bearing the new album's title. The retrospection continued within, as Visconti told *MOJO* magazine: 'Our biggest references were *Scary Monsters* and *Heathen*. Then we went back to the Berlin Trilogy, and there is a little bit of *The Man Who Sold the World* on this album too.' The title track bursts out of the gates, recalling both 'Beauty and the Beast' from *"Heroes"* and *Lodger*'s 'Repetition'. The remainder of the set drops similarly knowing references, from the 'Sound and Vision' keyboards of 'Love Is Lost' to the beat from 'Five Years' that closes out the twisted show-stopper 'You Feel So Lonely You Could Die'. There's an edginess and anxiety here, too, that evokes Bowie's early seventies recordings: a maverick gunman on the loose in the deceptively cheery 'Valentine's Day', soldiers in the Middle East in the psychedelically laced 'I'd Rather Be High', and apocalypse on 'Heat', the stark closer. In retrospect, some critics have found it patchy. Perhaps that knowingly self-referential stuff grated. In 2013, though, just having David Bowie back and enjoying himself seemed enough for most people.

In March that year Bowie aficionados queued in droves for the Victoria and Albert Museum's remarkable exhibition *David Bowie Is*, a blissfully in-depth retrospective of his life that took in stagewear, handwritten lyrics, instruments and Bowie's own art. Not long after it opened, the Dame himself popped in with his family during a holiday in Europe and surely admired its execution. It became the V&A's fast-est-selling show and subsequently went on a five-year tour of museums worldwide.

Released in 2014, the jazzy limited-edition single 'Sue (Or a Season in Crime)' introduced another change of pace and sound. It featured the tenor saxophonist Donny McCaslin (brought in at the suggestion of the bandleader Maria Schneider, whose jazz orchestra provided the backing), and acted as a taster for what would become Bowie's final album. The sessions for that set began in early 2015, with Visconti producing and support from McCaslin's small jazz combo, whom Bowie had caught at the tiny 55 Bar in Greenwich Village. All concerned were told to keep the sessions strictly secret, even signing non-disclosure forms. A few people in Bowie's circle knew that he now had cancer. By November he knew it was terminal.

With his remaining time and energy, Bowie laboured to finish something he'd never pulled off: a musical. Created with the playwright Enda Walsh and the musical director and arranger Henry Hey, *Lazarus* took as its main character Thomas Jerome Newton from *The Man Who Fell to Earth*, still stuck on Earth, alcoholic, guilt-ridden and longing for release. Packed with reworked songs from Bowie's past, it's a surreal jukebox musical in which characters are more conceptual, or indicative of emotional states, than fully realized people, and there's a blur between the objective world and what may be going through Newton's head. Some critics praised the cast and the imaginative production, although the convoluted plot frustrated many others. The show's initial New York run at the city's Theater Workshop, which began on 7 December 2015, sold out in three hours.

As with its predecessor, the 2016 album *Blackstar* dropped with no fanfare on Bowie's birthday, 8 January. Two days later the news broke that he had died.[1] Despite rumours about his ill health, it was inevitably a shock – he'd looked joyful and healthy, dressed in a sharp suit and fedora on the street, in photos posted online just two days earlier. He'd staged his public exit from the world with the panache that had characterized his best work, somehow contriving to keep both *Blackstar* and his own demise a secret from social media and, as with *The Next Day* in 2013 (both recorded in the heart of that most public of cities, New York), with no leaks from anyone involved, nor even a stray snapshot from a mobile phone. The album he left behind made for a remarkable farewell, peppered with references to his career – allusions more subtle than those on *The Next Day* – that became poignant in light of his death. ('Dollar Days' seemed to reveal intimations of mortality, but of acceptance too.) Right to the end, he kept fans and critics guessing, an artist whose work never revealed all.

The enigmas began with the album's stark black-and-white sleeve, with its cryptic typography – the only one of his solo albums not to feature his likeness. The darkly smooth 'Blackstar', with its droning Eastern motif set to a stuttering beat, shifts from melancholy minor to sunburst major. The title was richly suggestive, embracing the astronomical term for a stage between a collapsing star and a black hole, a cancer lesion and even a discarded song for an Elvis Presley Western.

An excerpt of the song was used for the opening theme of the crime drama *The Last Panthers*, which led to its director,

---

[1] After a private cremation, Bowie's ashes were scattered in Bali, in a Buddhist ritual.

Johan Renck, overseeing the album's two mesmerizing but unsettling videos. 'Blackstar' featured a spacesuit-clad skeleton whose bejewelled head becomes the focus of a ritual; dancers twitch and tremble; three scarecrows writhe on crucifixes in a field. Bowie, playing the last in a long line of characters stretching back to Ziggy Stardust, wears bandages on his head and has buttons for eyes, a persona he also referred to as the 'Blind Prophet', according to Visconti. The funereally paced 'Lazarus' projects him as a star in the firmament, singing of hidden scars – a reference to his illness, something more metaphysical, or both? The accompanying video again presents Bowie as Button Eyes, a haggard patient levitating above his hospital bed. It's bookended by the singer emerging from and then retreating to a wardrobe, clad in a replica of a striped outfit he'd posed in during the *Station to Station* era. In between, he writes furiously at a desk, with exaggerated gestures straight out of a silent movie, while his final retreat to the wardrobe precisely mirrors the movements of Cesare, the sleepwalking murderer in the classic German Expressionist horror film *The Cabinet of Dr Caligari*.

Bowie had drawn on Stanley Kubrick's *A Clockwork Orange* in creating his first great characterization, Ziggy Stardust, and on 'Girl Loves Me' he revisits the film's Nadsat lingo over a menacing backdrop. Elsewhere, the warm entry of the coda 'I Can't Give Everything Away' wafts in on a lilting harmonica that evokes both 'A New Career in a New Town' and 'Never Let Me Down'. It grows into a majestic closing statement. Throughout his shape-shifting career, Bowie had deliberately embraced artifice and fiction, changed his mind quickly and comprehensively, invented then discarded alter egos, spun myths. He'd started out one tour playing dystopian glam rock and finished it as a white (plastic) soul brother. His songs, he seems to be saying on *Blackstar*, mean whatever you, the listener, believe they mean. And the same held true for Bowie himself. 'I am only the person the greatest number of people believe that I am,' he'd said in 1994. Where is the joy in definitive meanings when the play of multiplicity is so rich with possibilities? Why live as one thing when there are so many different ways of being to explore? After all, David Bowie was simply the most famous of the masks that David Robert Jones wore.

Bowie's final album reaffirmed him as an unpredictable and unique presence in pop, the embodiment of Bob Dylan's line about artists not looking back. Repetition would have been unthinkable during his scintillating run from *The Man Who Sold the World* in 1971 to *Scary Monsters (And Super Creeps)* in 1980. And if he lost his way in the eighties, seduced by mainstream success, he had the nous to admit as much to himself, and to claw his way back to what he knew best – not unlike the man who shared his birthday, Elvis Presley, who enjoyed a musical renaissance at the close of the sixties by making an electrifying reconnection with his roots.

At the end Bowie was again working on instinct, finding fresh collaborators with whom to create a strange new sound, conjuring up another memorable image. Confounding expectations. Tantalizingly unknowable, just as in the old days. Then, like a great stage magician, he disappeared, leaving us rubbing our eyes, hungry for more.

David Bowie:
Album Discography

Studio albums

David Bowie (1967)

David Bowie (1969); later retitled *Space Oddity* (released as
   Man of Words, Man of Music in USA)

The Man Who Sold the World (1970)

Hunky Dory (1971)

The Rise and Fall of Ziggy Stardust and the Spiders from Mars (1972)

Aladdin Sane (1973)

Diamond Dogs (1974)

Young Americans (1975)

Station to Station (1976)

Low (1977)

"Heroes" (1977)

Lodger (1979)

Scary Monsters (And Super Creeps) (1980)

Let's Dance (1983)

Tonight (1984)

Never Let Me Down (1987)

Tin Machine (1989; as part of group)

Tin Machine II (1991; as part of group)

Black Tie White Noise (1993)

1. Outside (1995)

Earthling (1997)

'hours...' (1999)

Heathen (2002)

Reality (2003)

The Next Day (2013)

Blackstar (2016), aka ★

Live albums

David Live (1974)

Stage (1978)

Ziggy Stardust: the Motion Picture (1983)

Tin Machine Live: Oy Vey, Baby (1992; as part of group)

liveandwell.com (1999)

Glass Spider (2007)

Live Santa Monica '72 (2008)

A Reality Tour (2010)

Live Nassau Coliseum '76 (2017)

Cracked Actor (Live Los Angeles '74) (2017)

Live in Berlin (1978) (2018)

Welcome to the Blackout (Live London '78) (2018)

Serious Moonlight (Live '83) (2018)

Glastonbury 2000 (2018)

I'm Only Dancing (The Soul Tour '74) (scheduled for 2020)

Further Reading

Books

Broackes, Victoria, and Geoffrey Marsh (eds), *David Bowie Is* (London: V&A Publishing, 2013)

Buckley, David, *Strange Fascination – David Bowie: The Definitive Story* (London: Virgin, 2000)

Doggett, Peter, *The Man Who Sold the World: David Bowie and the 1970s* (London: Vintage, 2012)

Du Noyer, Paul, *In the City: A Celebration of London Music* (London: Virgin, 2010)

Dylan, Bob, *Chronicles: Volume One* (London: Pocket Books, 2005)

Goddard, Simon, *Ziggyology: A Brief History of Ziggy Stardust* (London: Ebury Press, 2013)

Green, Jonathon, *Days in the Life: Voices from the English Underground 1961–1971* (London: Minerva, 1988)

Hepworth, David, *Uncommon People: The Rise and Fall of Rock Stars* (London: Black Swan, 2017)

Jones, Dylan, *David Bowie: A Life* (London: Windmill Books, 2018)

Lancaster, Phil, *At the Birth of Bowie: Life with the Man Who Became a Legend* (London: John Blake Publishing, 2019)

Marsh, Dave, *Before I Get Old: The Story of the Who* (London: Plexus, 1983)

Napier-Bell, Simon, *Black Vinyl White Powder* (London: Ebury Press, 2002)

O'Leary, Chris, *Rebel: All of the Songs of David Bowie from '64 to '76* (London: Zero Books, 2015)

O'Leary, Chris, *Ashes to Ashes: The Songs of David Bowie 1976–2016* (London: Repeater, 2018)

Pegg, Nicholas, *The Complete David Bowie* (London: Titan Books, 2016)

Penman, Ian, *It Gets Me Home, This Curving Track* (London: Fitzcarraldo Editions, 2019)

Reynolds, Simon, *Shock and Awe: Glam Rock and its Legacy* (London: Faber & Faber, 2017)

Seabrook, Thomas Jerome, *Bowie in Berlin: A New Career in a New Town* (London: Jawbone Press, 2008)

Trynka, Paul, *Starman: David Bowie – The Definitive Biography* (London: Sphere, 2012)

Visconti, Tony, with Richard Havers, *Bowie, Bolan and the Brooklyn Boy* (London: HarperCollins, 2007)

Walden, George, and Jules Barbey d'Aurevilly, *Who's a Dandy? On Dandyism and Beau Brummell* (London: Gibson Square Books, 2002)

Wilde, Oscar, *Intentions: The Decay of Lying, Pen, Pencil and Poison, The Critic as Artist, The Truth of Masks* (New York: Brentano's, 1905)

Magazines

Primary sources: *Arena, Long Live Vinyl, MOJO, MOJO '60s, New Statesman* and *Uncut*

Websites

Of the wealth of Bowie-related sites available, I found the following consistently helpful: 5years.com, bowiebible.com, bowiegolden years.com, bowiesongs.wordpress.com and bowiewonderworld. com. For researching background material, archive.org proved a terrific resource.

Documentaries

Cracked Actor, dir. Alan Yentob (uncredited) for *Omnibus* series, BBC Television, 1975

David Bowie: Finding Fame, dir. Francis Whately, BBC Television, 2019

Index

Index

Index

Acknowledgements

With grateful thanks to my editors Donald Dinwiddie and Andrew Roff. Andrea and Tomi: thanks for your patience and support! Apa.

Picture Credits
(numbered in order of appearance)

1. Pictorial Press Ltd/Alamy

2. Photo via Kevin Cann/ Pictorial Press Ltd/Alamy

3. George Harris/*Evening News*/Shutterstock

4. Redferns/Getty Images

5. Ray Stevenson/Shutterstock

6. Trinity Mirror/Mirrorpix/Alamy

7. Michael Ochs Archives/Getty Images

8. Ilpo Musto/Shutterstock

9. Terry O'Neill/Getty Images

10. Pictorial Press Ltd/Alamy

11. Ron Galella/Wireimage/Getty Images

12, 13. Pictorial Press Ltd/Alamy

14. Michael Ochs Archives/Getty Images

15. Sheila Rock/Shutterstock

16. Pictorial Press Ltd/Alamy

17. Greg Mathieson/Shutterstock

18. Georges de Keerle/Getty Images

19. Kevin Mazur/Wireimage/Getty Images

20. David Bowie/VEVO